PRAISE FOR
IF JESUS LOVES ME WHY ISN'T THIS WORKING?

"I have never read anything like *If Jesus Loves Me Why Isn't This Working?* and I was fascinated by it. David Gregory has written an incredibly powerful yet easy way to know God's voice and His Word. This is a terrific and encouraging read for individuals and groups alike."

> —RALPH HARRIS, best-selling author of *Life According to Perfect: The Greatest Story Never Imagined* and *God's Outstanding Opinion of You: Understanding Your Identity Will Change Your Life*

"'I feel born again, again!' is the refrain many are singing at our church after reading David Gregory's latest book. Personally, after reading it the first time, I could not believe what I was reading. As a ministry leader and pastor for over 30 years, I had read all the scriptures contained in this book dozens of times. However, it wasn't until reading this book that the scriptures came alive again for me and I felt totally renewed! As I encountered Jesus on each page, I too felt as if I was being born again, again."

> —BRYAN THOMAS, Senior Pastor, Community Bible Church Highland Park, San Antonio

"As I read *If Jesus Loves Me Why Isn't This Working*, I experienced a calming peace and an uplifting joy, evidences that I was encountering God himself. You can, too, as David Gregory invites you into an intimate conversation with God who unfolds the truth about Christianity to you with such great clarity, you will discover the kind of Christian life you always hoped for. Reading this book could be one of the best decisions you've ever made!"

> —MARK MAULDING, best-selling author of *God's Best-Kept Secret*; president and founder of Grace Life International

"When I read *If Jesus Loves Me Why Isn't This Working?*, I realized that it is much more than a book. Rather, it is an invitation. An invitation to enter into the greatest Life you have ever known—your life as it was meant to be lived. Please accept the invitation. If you do, your life and your relationship with Jesus will be changed forever."

> —BILL LOVELESS, Director, Christ Is Life Ministries

"For a long time I didn't know how much God loved me. Even after I was told, I had trouble believing it. With good intentions, I had been struggling to try to love God more and didn't realize how much I first needed to be convinced of His love for me. This unique little book is the perfect 'recalibrator.'"

> —KARL A. KAKADELIS, Executive Director, Grace Ministries, Inc.

IF JESUS LOVES ME WHY ISN'T THIS WORKING?

DAVID GREGORY

ONE
PRESS

Katy, Texas

Cover design by Jenna Sue Bennett

Interior layout by Daria Lacy

Published by One Press, Katy, TX

www.davidgregorybooks.com

ISBN 0-9675141-3-4

9 8 7 6 5 4 3 2 1

Printed in the United States of America

To my mother, Wilma Ritter,
who has stood by me

CONTENTS

WHY ISN'T THIS WORKING?

The worst Christian ever. That's what I called myself. Not to others, of course. To everyone else, I presented the face you're supposed to present: everything's fine. Life is great.

But everything wasn't fine, and life wasn't great. I'd been laid off from my job 14 months before and had been making ends meet, barely, doing consulting work when I could find it. We had run through our cash savings and then through most of our retirement savings. My wife Elise and I had had a pretty good marriage. Now we fought too often. My 14 year old Jeff's grades had gone from As to Cs and Ds since his first girlfriend dumped him. Elise and Emily, our 13 year old, were always at odds with each other. I had unpaid medical bills from my hernia surgery. Every day I felt constant financial pressure.

"But that's not the worst of it," I admitted to Tim Cropp, my best friend for years, one Saturday morning at Starbucks. We met there weekly just to catch up and, occasionally, talk about our plans to be better men. If sitting at Starbucks talking about how to be a better person actually made you a better person, I'd be the best guy on the planet. But it doesn't. And I wasn't.

"The worst," I admitted to Tim, "is my reaction to it all. I get angry. I yell at the kids. I'm moody. I'm sharp with Elise. I honestly don't think she even wants to be married anymore. I wouldn't if I were her."

Tim let out a snort. "Dylan, Elise doesn't want to get a divorce. I don't believe that. Financial problems, kid stuff . . . they're hard on every marriage."

I looked down at my caramel latte. *If I keep ordering these things, they'll eventually have to wheel me out of here.* "It's just that she expected so much more. I was someone she looked up to. Older. Further down the road with God. That's what attracted her to me."

"I thought she was attracted to your muscles," Tim interjected.

"Yeah, right. It's like . . . back then I *was* spiritual. Or at least I thought so. Now, God has abandoned me or something. It's like he's punishing me."

A couple in their twenties took the table next to us, the last open one. The place filled up pretty quickly on Saturdays.

"Punishing you for what?" Tim asked.

"For not putting him first. For being out of fellowship with him all the time. I don't know."

"What's taking you out of fellowship?"

"Wrong thoughts. Wrong attitudes. Not being loving to my family. Getting mad in traffic. Not spending time with God regularly. You know—we've talked about all of this."

Tim sighed. "Are you talking about your life or mine?"

"Yeah, but God isn't punishing you. All the devotional times and prayer and Bible studies—honestly, what good has it all done? It doesn't stop me from failing all the time. I'm a terrible example for my children. I don't love my wife as selflessly as I should. I'm not a good witness for Christ."

Tim's brow furrowed. "You're being way too hard on yourself. You're a good dad. I've seen you with the kids a million times. And you're a good husband." He smiled sarcastically. "For the most part."

I shook my head. "I'm just not good enough for God. I'm embarrassed to come to him anymore. I feel like I need to get my act together to return to him. But what hope do I have of doing that? I've done all the Christian things. What's the point of gearing up some big effort again to try to become more spiritual? I'll just fail. God never answers my prayers. I never really hear from him. I never get anything out of it anymore when I read the Bible. Nothing's ever going to get any better. Whatever Jesus meant by 'abundant life,' I've missed it—for this life at least."

"Look, you're just going through a rough stretch," Tim replied. "What do they call it? The dark night of the soul."

Dark night of the soul? My life was more like living on the dark side of the moon. As far as I could tell, I'd never see sunlight again. I knew some people endured a lot worse circumstances than I was going through. But that's not much consolation when the problems are yours.

Tim and I stared at each other. I knew I couldn't say anything that would make him think horribly of me—he knew me far too well for that. And I realized that when I got down, I did have a tendency to see everything just a bit negatively. Tim had never heard me this low, though.

"I'm desperate," I finally admitted. "Whatever this Christian life is supposed to provide—whatever Jesus promised—I have to have it. I know where all this is heading, and it isn't good. I'm serious, what I said about my marriage. How long is Elise going to stay with someone who lives like this year after year? And the kids ... they're going to do exactly what most other kids from church families do when they go to college. They're going to abandon their faith, because they don't see it making a difference in the lives of their parents. And as for me, I don't know how much longer I can play this game. The Bible promises one thing and my life, no matter how hard I try, doesn't come close to matching up. Is any of this Christian thing real? Do you ever ask yourself that?"

Tim nodded slowly. "Yeah. Sometimes I do. I just never admit it to anyone."

"I just don't get it," I continued. "If Jesus loves me so much, why isn't any of this working?"

He shrugged. "I wish I had an answer for you. An answer for both of us."

"I know. Me too."

We were silent for a moment before Tim spoke. "Look, I'm here for you." He glanced at his cell phone. "Well, I will be here for you when I get back in three months."

Tim's company was sending him to Abu Dhabi for an extended assignment. He had done it before, and he said it wasn't that bad. Right. The more he insisted it was OK, the more miserable it sounded. Although getting paid extra for going overseas sounded nice. Actually, getting paid at all sounded nice.

"When is your flight?" I asked.

"Not till tonight. But I have to finish packing."

"I have to help Elise finish packing," I echoed.

"Where is she going?"

"Taking the kids to see their grandparents for three weeks in North Carolina."

"Didn't they do that last year?"

"Every year."

"And you don't go?"

I smiled. "They need the bonding time. Plus I've got contract work I can't put off." I glanced at the time. "I've got to run by a motor repair business I'm setting up a computer system for."

"See?" Tim said. "Business is picking up."

"Yeah, right."

He finished off his coffee. "Look, I don't feel like I've been much help."

"It helps for you just to listen." Isn't that what I was supposed to say?

"I'm praying for you, you know." He grabbed his keys and stood up. "Maybe by the time I get back I'll have the answer."

I rolled my eyes. "Just email me from over there when you do. As if I haven't heard it all before."

We said our goodbyes and Tim headed out the door. I scooted my chair back a bit, sighed, and finished my latte while looking at the morning headlines on my phone. As I did, a voice came from the table behind me.

"Excuse me."

I turned around to face an older guy, probably in his mid-sixties, sitting at the next table by himself.

"Sorry," he said, "it's hard not to hear conversations in here. Did you say that you set up computer networks?"

"Yes, I do." I straightened up a little to at least try to look professional. Which was hard to do in my shorts and T-shirt.

He pulled out a business card and handed it to me.

FRANK PULLMAN

OWNER AND CERTIFIED FINANCIAL PLANNER

PULLMAN FINANCIAL SERVICES

"My business is moving to a new location and we need someone to do just that. Can you give me a call Monday?"

"Sure," I replied. I pulled out one of my own cards and gave it to him. "Be glad to." That had never happened to me before, finding a random business prospect at Starbucks.

I worked a few hours before heading home to help Elise pack. The kids were already complaining about the trip.

"Three weeks!" Emily moaned. "What are we going to do at Grandma and Grandpa's for three weeks?"

"You'll get a great tan at the beach," Elise replied.

I drove the three of them to the airport late in the afternoon, walked them to the security checkpoint, and gave them hugs and kisses. "I'll miss you!" I told them. Which was true. The peace and quiet would be great for a day or two. Then I'd get lonely and bored. And with Tim gone, what, other than contract work, was I going to do for three weeks? Go to Astros games by myself?

It was dusk as I drove home, parked in the driveway, and walked up to the front door. There I saw something unusual.

A large manila envelope was leaning against the door frame. My name was handwritten on the outside:

Dylan Cooke

There was no return address. I picked it up and opened it. Inside was a piece of paper. I pulled it out. A single sentence was handwritten on it.

Do you want Me to teach you?

TWO

THE INVITATION

What exactly was I supposed to do with this piece of paper? Someone had put this envelope on my front porch while I had gone to the airport. Surely it wasn't here when we all left. And this someone was … what? Claiming to speak for God? For Jesus? Isn't that what the capital *M* in *Me* meant?

Who would claim such a thing? And what exactly did they imagine I needed to be taught? I took it inside, sat down at the breakfast table, and stared at it. The writing wasn't Elise's. I had never seen this handwriting before, as far as I knew. The whole thing was kind of weird. I did with it what I had done with most of the mail that had arrived that day. I threw it away.

On Tuesday I was in Frank Pullman's office, meeting his three employees and determining what his needs were for a new computer setup. He invited me to lunch after I had finished my assessment. He was, I discovered, a believer in Christ. And a man whom, as we got to know each other a bit, I quickly came to admire. There was a certain quality about him that I couldn't quite put my finger on, but that I couldn't help but be impressed by. He was at peace. At rest on the inside. I don't know why, but I could just tell.

After lunch I drove home and pulled into the driveway. And sat, staring. There it was—another manila envelope leaning against the front door. I got out and opened it. It held a single piece of paper. The handwriting was the same as before.

Do you want Me to teach you?

Who in the world was putting these envelopes on my front doorstep? My church? They wouldn't ever do this. My neighbors? I suppose they could, but why? I went inside and racked my brain. I just didn't have any good candidates. Not that there *were* any good candidates for this sort of thing.

I didn't throw this sheet away. Maybe I'd need it for handwriting analysis or fingerprint analysis or something. I just slid it into a drawer where I kept papers to file.

When Elise called that night, I didn't mention it, just as I hadn't mentioned the first one. What was I supposed to say? "Anonymous envelopes, allegedly from Jesus, are arriving at our doorstep"? She'd think I was crazy. Or just worry herself to death. There was no point putting her through that.

Two days later I started installing the computer network at Frank's business. I spent the better part of Thursday and Friday there, working on the network and chatting with Frank. I even ventured to share some of my struggles with him—financial, marital, even spiritual. I'm not sure what prompted me to do that. Maybe it was Elise and Tim being away at the same time. I didn't really have anyone else to talk to. And Frank just seemed … safe. He listened intently without automatically giving a bunch of advice. I appreciated that.

"Do you think God speaks to people today?" I asked him as I was taking a break toward the end of Friday.

"Of course."

"How?"

"Well, through his Word. Through other people. By his Spirit directly, to our spirit."

I sipped on the Dr Pepper I had grabbed from his fridge. "Has God ever spoken to you audibly?"

"No. He could if he wanted to."

"Has he ever written you a note?"

Frank laughed. "That would be something, wouldn't it?"

I smiled. "Yeah, it would."

It would indeed.

Saturday morning I went out and ran some errands. When I got back home, another envelope was waiting for me at the front door. I opened it. Two words had been added.

Do you want Me to teach you or not?

By Monday I made a decision. I had to tell *someone*. I needed someone's feedback, a person I could trust. Tim was still just getting set up in Abu Dhabi, I presumed. I didn't want to burden him with this. And I still didn't want to make Elise start worrying. So …

I pushed the latest manila envelope with its sheet of paper across Frank's desk to him. "This is the third one of these I've received in the last week. Always leaning on my front door."

He looked at it, turned it over and looked on the blank back side. "They all said the same thing?"

"Well, this one added *or not*."

He smiled. "Do you think Jesus is getting impatient?"

"I think someone's playing a prank on me. Why, I don't know."

He handed it back to me. "Seems like an odd prank."

"I'll say."

He leaned back in his office chair and put his hands behind his head. "Maybe it's not a prank."

"What do you mean?"

"Maybe God has something to say to you."

"What? That's ridiculous. God doesn't speak this way."

He shrugged. "It seems to me he can speak however he wants to. Maybe he's writing you a note and putting it at your door. Or maybe one of his people is writing you a note and putting it at your door. What's the difference?"

I was still thinking about the absurdity of the situation. It took a second for what Frank had said to sink in. "Huh? What do you mean, what's the difference? There's a huge difference."

He leaned forward, arms on his desk. "Look, if Christ lives in us, then he is living through us. And whether he chooses to use one of us to write a message to you, or if he writes you a personalized letter, there's really not much difference, as far as I can see. Either way, it's him sending you a message."

I sat back in my chair and soaked that in for a minute. "I guess I just don't want to be made a fool of."

He grinned. "Too late. We're all fools for Christ."

"So you think I should take Jesus—or whoever it is—up on this?"

"I would. Who knows what God may have in store."

I drove home, mowed the lawn, watched the Astros on TV, and Skyped with Elise and the kids. They looked sunburned. Before going to bed, I pulled out a blank sheet of printer paper and wrote a single word on it.

OK

I put it in an envelope and left it on the doorstep.

THREE

LESSONS

The next morning, I was checking the front doorstep about every 15 minutes. Maybe it was foolish to so eagerly anticipate another mystery envelope, but I couldn't help it. *Who knows, maybe these things really are from God.* Just after 8:30 I opened the front door again. There was another envelope. Inside was a handwritten note, just like before.

> *Dylan, here's your first lesson. Plus some questions for you to answer.*

It wasn't signed. The other pages hadn't been either.

I was still skeptical, to say the least. I walked back into the house, sat down at the breakfast table, and read the two pages. They were … thought provoking. In fact, they were unlike anything I had read before. Could this really be from Jesus? It didn't exactly contradict everything I thought I knew. But it didn't really match it, either.

Frank and I had arranged to meet for lunch that afternoon. I had already finished setting up his computer network. We were meeting because, well, I just wanted to. I handed him the two pages. He read them.

"What do you think?" I asked.

He handed them back to me. "I agree with every word on there."

I examined his face. He examined mine. I had already run through my mind what had happened the first time I met Frank at Starbucks. He had given me his business card. I had given him mine. My home address was on it. I had left Starbucks to go to the motor repair shop for a few hours. I had returned to find an envelope on my front porch.

I asked him the logical question. "Are you leaving these envelopes at my door?"

He smiled. I expected a *Yes* or a *No*. What I didn't expect was his actual response.

"I'm not going to tell you," he said. "As I said before, if God is writing these to you directly, they are from him. And if they are from me or someone else—well, Christ is the one living in us, isn't he?" He had a bite of a fajita wrap before continuing. "Either way, I would just ask God, what are you saying to me here?"

So I did. I went home and read the pages again. And again. And again. And I waited for the next lesson. I just assumed something new would show up shortly. But nothing did. Had I done something wrong? Did Jesus want me to first apply what I had already read? Honestly, I wasn't sure how to apply it. It wasn't really an application-oriented thing.

I waited two more days. Then, another envelope. I opened it immediately. It wasn't a new lesson, but only a one-sentence handwritten note.

I'm waiting for your answers.

Waiting for my answers? What did—and then it dawned on me. There had been some questions. Maybe I was supposed to write down my answers and put them back in the envelope. I made a copy of the first lesson, wrote my answers on the copy, and put them in an envelope on the front porch.

The next day another lesson arrived. I read it, wrote my answers to the questions, and put them back in the envelope. Three days later another lesson came. I had received four by the time Elise and the kids got back.

My first inclination, of course, was to tell Elise immediately what had been happening with the envelopes. God was speaking to me! On the way to the airport, I changed my mind. If God was speaking to me, I decided, it should become apparent. There should be changes. I already felt like things were changing for me, but I wanted to see if she would notice.

About two weeks after she got back, she commented. "Dylan, what happened to you while I was gone? I've never seen you so excited about your relationship with God."

I pulled out the notes and the lessons and showed them to her.

She stared at them incredulously. "So these have been showing up at the front door?"

"Yep."

"And you think Jesus is actually sending them to you?"

"I think Jesus is speaking to me. Who is putting these envelopes by the front door, I don't know."

She looked back down at the lessons and continued reading one. Then the next. Then the next. I slipped onto a barstool and simply waited.

"Well," she finally said, "whoever is delivering them, they're amazing. I've never read anything like this. Why didn't someone tell us this before?"

I shrugged. "Maybe we weren't ready to hear it yet."

She put the papers down and gave me a long kiss. "Well, I'm just glad you said *OK*."

"I am too."

The lessons kept coming. Frank and I kept meeting for lunch. I would make copies of the lessons for him and we would discuss them over fajitas.

"My life has completely changed," I admitted to him after a couple of months. "My relationship with God has completely changed."

He smiled. "I can tell."

"I don't look at anything the way I used to. And I didn't do anything, really. I just . . . I just did what the lessons told me to do. Which was—well, you've read them."

"What about for Elise? You told me she's been reading them."

"Exactly the same. Her relationship with God has been transformed."

"And how about your marriage?" he asked, a twinkle in his eye.

I grinned. "That's improved as well."

I dipped a chip in salsa. "What these lessons have taught me—you already knew about these things, didn't you?"

He nodded.

"For how long?"

"Twenty years. Maybe 25."

"And who told you them?"

"Jesus did."

I stopped my next bite. "Jesus did? You mean, you got these same kind of letters—"

He laughed. "No, not at all."

"So where did you get this stuff?"

"From the Bible. Jesus just started showing me from the Bible."

I felt confused. "But I've spent lots of time in the Bible. Why didn't he do that with me? Why did he write out these lessons?"

Frank shook his head. "I have no idea. But I know this: God often does what he does in us, because he wants to do something through us. Maybe Jesus gave you these lessons because he wants you to do something with them."

I thought about Tim, due to arrive back in the States in a month. "I'm going to give them to Tim when he returns. I know he's pretty much been where I was before all of this— trying hard to be a good Christian, but never quite getting there."

Frank nodded again. "I can believe that. That's where pretty much everyone is, aren't they?"

"I'm guessing he'd love to know what Jesus has taught me."

Frank picked up another chip. "I'm guessing he would. But let me ask you this: is there anyone you wouldn't want to share these lessons with? Anyone you wouldn't want to know these things?"

That didn't take much thought to answer. "No. Absolutely not. I want everyone to know."

And suddenly it became so apparent. I was God's conduit. Jesus was in me, wanting me to share with others exactly what he had shared with me.

So I am. Here's what Jesus taught me.

... the good news of the glory of the happy God. (1 Timothy 1:11)

We write this to you so you can be full of joy with us. (1 John 1:4)

CREATED FOR LOVE

This life—the life that I have given you—is simple. It is so simple, in fact, that you have to be like a little child to receive it. That's what I told my disciples, remember?

But sometimes the simplest things need to be explained, because they seem complicated at first. That's what this life seems like to you: complicated. But it's not. It's the simplest thing.

Before we start, I want to let you know that I won't be saying a single thing in these lessons that is new. I've already said it all in the book you call the Bible. I breathed that book through people who knew me. It lasts forever, and my Spirit teaches you through it. Unfortunately, what it plainly says has, in many cases, been obscured under layers of human reasoning. As a result, what should be as clear as day, isn't.

As we go through these lessons, I will include in each one what I said before in the Bible. As you look at what I said before, it will be clear that what I'm saying here is not new. Nothing needs to be said that hasn't been said previously. You simply need to *hear* it freshly.

Here's how I want to begin: as if you and I had not yet met one another. If we start where you are right now, we have to sort through a lot of misconceptions and misunderstandings. These have produced your current frustration.

It's understandable that you are frustrated. You hear me say, "I came that they might have abundant life," and you are thinking, "Great. Where is it?" Your frustration is not without purpose. It has opened your heart to what I want to teach you now.

He ... is the blessed and only Sovereign, the King of kings and Lord of lords, who alone possesses immortality and dwells in unapproachable light, whom no man has seen or can see. (1 Timothy 6:15-16)

For by Him all things were created ... He is before all things, and in Him all things hold together. (Colossians 1:16-17)

In Him was life ... (John 1:4)

My plan for you from eternity past is greater than you know, and things have already happened to you—wonderful things— that you haven't fully understood. So let's back up. Let's start at the beginning, as if you and I don't know each other at all. That way we can lay a proper foundation. And you will see how simple this life really is.

Here, then, is what I would say to you, who don't yet know me.

My name is I Am That I Am. I created the universe, but I am unlike anything in it.

I am perfect love.

I am infinite power.

I am infinite knowledge.

I am perfect holiness.

I have no beginning and no end.

I am everywhere.

I hold the seemingly endless universe in the palm of my hand, and it is as nothing before me. Yet I made it with perfect precision and care for and sustain it in tender love. I sustain you with tender love.

Among all of my creation, I designed one being in my own image, with the capacity to imagine, to create, to choose, to love, and, above all, to know me. You are that being. And what I created you to be is amazing.

I didn't create you to join a religious institution.

I didn't create you to perform religious duties.

I didn't create you to follow lists of rules.

I didn't create you to deny you anything good.

I didn't create you to be anxious, or guilt-ridden, or bitter, or stressed.

God is love. (1 John 4:8)

"I have loved you with an everlasting love ..."
(Jeremiah 31:3)

I didn't create you to be unfulfilled or incomplete.
I didn't even create you primarily to get you into heaven.
Here's what I *did* create you for:

*I created you to share in, and
forever enjoy, and show to the
universe, the overflowing life and
love of the infinitely happy God.*

How?
In a way you have likely never imagined.
But first I want to tell you something else, something very important:

You are eternally, infinitely loved.

You have heard that I am love, and you have assumed that my love is like human love, only a bit better. Human love is almost always conditional. Behave well enough, and you will be loved by people. Behave poorly enough and their love will fade.

But my love is *nothing* like human love. My love is unconditional. Your performance doesn't affect it in the least. Your performance can't affect it, because love isn't just something that I do. It is who I am. I am love. I love you because it's my nature to love you. I keep on loving you, no matter what your behavior is, because it's my nature to love you.

The closest humans ever come to this kind of love is the love of a parent for a newborn baby. The baby does nothing to earn being loved. She cannot really love in return. She is loved simply because she is. My love for you is like that, only infinitely more so. You are loved simply because you are.

My love is like the ocean. If you are in the ocean, you can't escape the wet. It surrounds you. It envelopes you. There is

In this is love, not that we loved God, but that he loved us ... (1 John 4:10)

nowhere to go where it isn't with you. My love surrounds you, envelopes you, is always with you.

My love is like the air in the earth's atmosphere, miles deep, that presses down upon you. You can't escape it. You can't do anything to make it go away. My love always presses upon you.

When you were mean for the first time to one of your childhood playmates, I was there loving you. When you disobeyed your mother or father, and lied, and deceived, I was there loving you. When you scorned a friend for the sake of an offer that seemed more appealing, I was there loving you. When you suffered the bad consequences of your actions, and felt devastated, I was there loving you. And when you were badly hurt by someone close to you, I was there loving you, and hurting with you.

I was loving you because that's who I am.

In love I created you. In love I sustain you. In love I have designed you for something incredible. And in love I have done everything needed to make that a reality—at a very great cost to myself. What is that incredible something? I will tell you.

"... that they may all be one [with us], just as you, Father, are in me, and I in you, that they also may be in us ... I in them and you in me ..." (John 17:21, 23)

"In that day you will know that I am in My Father, and you in Me, and I in you."
— *Jesus (John 14:20)*

The one who joins himself to the Lord is one spirit with Him. (1 Corinthians 6:17)

"I have made Your name known to them, and will make it known, so that the love with which You loved Me may be in them, and I in them."
— *prayer of Jesus (John 17:26)*

LESSON 2

CREATED FOR ONENESS

The Eastern religions have it right: the goal of the universe, of existence, is oneness with the Ultimate. But it's not the oneness they imagine: merging with an impersonal universal force in which you lose all your individuality, all your personality—all that makes you, you. There is no good news in that. Rather,

*you were created to
be one with me,*

the infinitely loving, infinitely happy God.

But what does being one with me mean? It means your human spirit is actually joined to me, becoming so united that we are one. Not that you lose who you are. You will always be you, the person I created you to be. Rather, just as male and female are temporarily united in flesh, your spirit is meant to be permanently united to me. This is what you were created for. I am spirit, and you were created in my image, for your spirit to be one with me.

Once you are united to me, my life is actually infused into you. I come to live in your spirit. And I bring who I am into your heart: love, peace, joy, inner rest.

Think of the stress you experience, the conflict, the anxiety, the striving. Do any of those feel like you were created for them? No? That's because you weren't created for them! You were made for so much more. You weren't made to strive to make life work or to attain the right behavior. Rather, you

... the mystery which has been hidden from the past ages and generations, but has now been manifested ... which is Christ in you ... (Colossians 1:26-27)

"... I came that they may have life, and have it abundantly." — Jesus (John 10:10)

were made to be joined to me, so that I live my perfect, loving life through you. You become the expression of me to all the universe.

That is oneness with me. That is what you were created for. It is an eternal adventure beyond your wildest dreams, and is the source of meaning and fulfillment beyond anything this world has to offer.

That's the incredibly good news.

This is what I intended humans to be from the very beginning. But humanity chose another path. It chose to try to make life work on its own, apart from me, its true source of life. That choice plunged humanity into darkness, selfishness, rebellion, and a desperate search for meaning.

Don't you see this in the world around you? The divisions, the strife, the hatred, the rage, the selfishness, the bitterness, the stress, the anxiety, the envy, the tearing down of everything meant to be good—this is not the way humans were intended to be. Isn't it obvious that something has gone very wrong?

You see this in your own life as well. You may have made a fairly nice life for yourself in the here and now, but deep down, you know something is amiss. Your heart tugs at you. You were meant for something higher. You were meant to be connected to Someone greater. Everyone, in the depths of their heart, knows this to be true.

You were made to be connected to, to be brought into, an eternal community of love. That is what we are. God the Father. God the Son. God the Holy Spirit. We have never been alone. We have been loving one another, delighting in one another, for all eternity. We made you to be part of our community of perfect, limitless love. Forever. This is your true home, your only home. This is what you were created for: to know, and receive, and live in the infinite love of God.

Thanks be to God for His indescribable gift!
(2 Corinthians 9:15)

The religions of the world offer their rules and rituals, and through them people try to work their way back to God. But no rules and no rituals can accomplish that. How are rules and rituals going to make you one with us? It's impossible. Becoming one with us is never, ever something you can achieve. Making you one with us is something only I can do for you.

So I offer this—oneness with us—to you as a gift. It isn't something you can earn. It isn't something you have to strive for. I simply give it to you. It is everything you were designed for, everything your heart longs for, everything you could possibly need and even want, forever.

You have but a single part to play. You must choose to receive it.

I will tell you how.

But first, I must tell you what I have done, and what I do, to make this wonder, being joined to us, a reality. *I myself* do everything necessary to bring you back to us, and enable you to be what we created you to be.

There is none righteous, not even one ... for all have sinned and fall short of the glory of God. (Romans 3:10, 23)

"This is the judgment, that the Light has come into the world, and men loved the darkness rather than the light, for their deeds were evil." — Jesus (John 3:19)

For we also once were foolish ourselves, disobedient, deceived, enslaved to various lusts and pleasures, spending our life in malice and envy, hateful, hating one another. (Titus 3:3)

LESSON 3

TO MAKE US ONE, I TAKE AWAY WHAT SEPARATES US

B ecause of my great love for you, it was my plan from eternity past to be joined to you forever. It's what I created you for. But two things interfered with that plan. I had to take care of them both for you.

The first was the issue of your sins. A penalty had to be paid for your sins. Sins are simply the things you do, or say, or the attitudes you have, that are wrong. That is, the things that fall short of my perfection.

That's a very high standard. An impossible one. Couldn't I just ignore some of the more minor violations? Many people believe, and some religions teach, that if they simply do enough good things I will overlook their bad things. That is false. It is false for two reasons.

First, just as I am perfect love, I am perfectly just. You wouldn't want it any other way. Would you want the universe run by Someone who is unjust? Being perfectly just, I cannot simply sweep sins under the rug or grade on the curve. The penalty for any violation must be paid.

Second, it is false because it drastically understates the significance of sin. Sin violates the entire moral order of the universe. Let me show you why.

I am love. What that means is that I am other-love, for that is what love is, being for others, not self. You were created to be joined to, and express, my perfect, other-loving life. That is the source of all fulfillment, all contentment, all meaning, and

But God demonstrates His own love for us, in that while we were yet sinners, Christ died for us. (Romans 5:8)

In this is love: not that we have loved God, but that he loved us and sent his Son to be the atoning sacrifice for our sins. (1 John 4:10)

For Christ also died for sins once for all, the just for the unjust, so that He might bring us to God ... (1 Peter 3:18)

true harmony and peace among all people.

But humanity chose to seek life on its own terms, to look for life and meaning and significance apart from me. In doing so, it became entirely self-seeking. This was rebellion against the entire moral order. It is the opposite of who I am and who I created you to be. It plunged humanity into darkness. Everything you see wrong with the world around you resulted.

In choosing this path, humanity separated itself from me. It wasn't my choice. It was yours. Sin separated humanity from me. Do you see how no one escapes this reality? Everyone is guilty.

So sin carries its own penalty—not only of present separation from me, but of continual separation from me. That penalty had to be paid. And if an individual person paid for his or her own sins, it would mean separation from me forever.

But I have loved you forever. And I created you not for eternal separation, but for eternal oneness with me. So I made a choice that only I could make. I would take your penalty upon myself.

I am God. God the Son. Being the Creator, I am greater than the creation. And so I, and I alone, was able to pay for the sins of all of humanity.

This why God the Father sent me, Jesus Christ, to earth: to die on a cross, to pay the penalty for the sins of all humanity, so that your slate could be wiped clean. Because of love, I died in your place. I took the punishment. On the cross I became sin itself. I was separated from the Father. I took on myself the penalty I did not owe, so that you would not have to.

I didn't come primarily to be a great teacher, or a great example, though those things are important. I came to die and be resurrected in your place. I came to pay the highest possible price for your sins.

As a result, we offer you complete forgiveness. You can be

41

For the wages of sin is death, but the free gift of God is eternal life in Christ Jesus our Lord. (Romans 6:23)

made completely right with God, as if you had never sinned at all. There is nothing you have to do to earn it. There is nothing you *can* do to earn it. It is purely a gift. All you have to do is receive it.

Receiving forgiveness is not an end in itself, however. It is simply what had to be done first to accomplish the true goal of making you and us one.

You were dead in your trespasses and sins, in which you formerly walked according to the course of this world, according to ... the spirit that is now working in the sons of disobedience. Among them we too all formerly lived in the lusts of our flesh, indulging the desires of the flesh and of the mind, and were by nature children of wrath, even as the rest. (Ephesians 2:1-3)

... you were at that time separate from Christ ... having no hope and without God in the world. (Ephesians 2:12)

[Living] in the futility of their mind, being darkened in their understanding, excluded from the life of God because of the ignorance that is in them, because of the hardness of their heart ... (Ephesians 4:17-18)

TO MAKE US ONE, I GIVE YOU A HEART TRANSPLANT

Once I forgive your sins, a second issue remains, larger than the first. It is this: sins arise from a heart that is cut off from me. Humanity chose to go its own independent way, rebelling against me, its source of true life and goodness. As a result, every person is born with a rebel heart, committed to its own way. To put it another way, every person is born with a spirit dead to me, cut off from my life and unresponsive to me.

On the outside, this heart may look to be in real rebellion, indulging in various of the worst-looking sins. Or it may appear completely respectable, being a good citizen, a good employee, a good spouse, a good parent, even a good church-goer. The issue isn't the manner in which this heart expresses its true nature. The issue is that this heart, however it appears to operate in the world, doesn't have life. I am life. In the depths of their inner being, people are born dead. They are dead to me.

For you and me to be one—for you to be what you were created to be—your heart has to be given life. I am life. I must be joined to your heart. But I can't join myself to a spirit in rebellion against me. I am perfectly holy. I can't eternally join myself to something that is unholy. Your heart must be changed.

The problem is that you can't do anything to make your heart better. It's a rebel spirit, and it will always be a rebel spirit, committed to its own way. The only solution is for me to give you a heart transplant. And that is exactly what I do. I remove your old, sinful heart. I don't try to make it better. It can't be made

"I will give you a new heart and put a new spirit within you; and I will remove the heart of stone from your flesh and give you a heart of flesh." (Ezekiel 36:26)

"Unless one is born again [from above] he cannot see the kingdom of God ... Unless one is born of water and the Spirit he cannot enter into the kingdom of God. That which is born of the flesh is flesh, and that which is born of the Spirit is spirit." — Jesus (John 3:3, 5, 6)

Knowing this, that our old self was crucified with Him ... (Romans 6:6)

The new self ... in the likeness of God has been created in righteousness and holiness of the truth. (Ephesians 4:24)

Therefore if anyone is in Christ, he is a new creation; the old things passed away; behold, new things have come. Now all things are from God ... (2 Corinthians 5:17, 18)

better. I simply take it out. I promised this to the Hebrews long ago. Under a completely new arrangement with humanity, I said, "I will remove the heart of stone from your flesh."

Your old heart, committed to a path of destruction, cut off from its source of true life—I literally remove it from you. But when an old heart is removed, it must be replaced by a new heart. And that is what I do to you. I give you an entirely new heart. My Spirit actually births within you a new human spirit. As I explained to Nicodemus, a religious leader in his day, that which is born of the flesh—of human bodies through procreation—is flesh, and that which is born of the Spirit is spirit. So I told him, "You must be born again."

To become one with me, you must have both a human birth *and* a birth from my Spirit. Once you do, your heart is fully ready to be joined. That's because your new spirit is just like me—completely holy and righteous. And is it any wonder? You are now born of me. You are born from above, by my Spirit. And my Spirit cannot give birth to anything that is not completely holy and righteous, as I am. Those who are born of the Spirit now truly come from God.

I told the Hebrews that under my new arrangement with humanity, I would give people a full heart transplant, taking out the old heart and putting in the new: "I will give you a new heart and put a new spirit within you; and I will remove the heart of stone from your flesh and give you a heart of flesh."

Once you are born from above, your new heart is fully prepared to be joined to me, because it is birthed by my Spirit. Now you are ready for what I created you for.

So forgiving your sins, removing your old heart, and giving you a new heart are necessary steps. But they are merely steps. They are not themselves the ultimate goal.

I will tell you next what is.

The one who joins himself to the Lord is one spirit with Him. (1 Corinthians 6:17)

"In that day you will know that I am in My Father, and you in Me, and I in you."
— Jesus (John 14:20)

"I will give you a new heart and put a new spirit within you; and I will remove the heart of stone from your flesh and give you a heart of flesh. I will put my Spirit within you ..."
(Ezekiel 36:26)

TO MAKE US ONE, I JOIN MYSELF TO YOU FOREVER

The ultimate goal is the very last thing I asked the Father to do before I started toward the cross. I asked him to make you one with me, and with him.

The Father *always* answers the Son's prayers.

I didn't come to earth just so your sins could be forgiven. I came to bring you into oneness with us. Having given you a new spirit, we then join ourselves to you in a one-spirit, eternal union. You become one with us, just as we are one with one another. As God, the three of us have an eternal union. An eternal fellowship of perfect love. The Father is in the Son and Spirit. The Son is in the Father and Spirit. The Spirit is in the Father and Son.

Now, you become one with us. We live inside you. You live inside us. We are one with you. You are one with us. You are brought into the very heart of our union with one another. Here, there is no space between us. We are one.

This joining is permanent. It cannot be undone. Your behavior, whatever it may be, cannot unmake it. Your doubts cannot undo it. We are one forever. Nothing can separate you from us. Nothing can separate you from our perfect fellowship of love. Everything that the infinitely happy God has, and is, is now yours. Now all things belong to you, and you belong to us. Just as I intended, from before the creation of the world.

You aren't accustomed to living within such perfect love. You aren't accustomed to every one of your needs already

IF JESUS LOVES ME WHY ISN'T THIS WORKING?

But as many as received Him, to them He gave the right to become children of God, even to those who believe in His name, who were born, not of blood nor of the will of the flesh nor of the will of man, but of God. (John 1:12-13)

For by grace you have been saved through faith, and that not of yourselves, it is the gift of God, not as a result of works, that no one should boast. (Ephesians 2:8, 9)

being met. You aren't used to experiencing joy that can't be quenched, peace that transcends difficulties, love that flows out even to those who are unlovely. You aren't accustomed to reigning with me over all of the universe, for all of eternity.

That's OK. You'll become accustomed to it. It's who we are.

But first, you and we must become one. In that, you have one part to play. You must receive it.

How do you receive what I am offering? It's very simple.

But I want you to remember that making you one with me is entirely my work. You can't make it happen. It doesn't happen by you being good enough. It doesn't happen by you keeping most of what you imagine are my rules, or performing religious rituals. It doesn't happen by what you do or don't eat, how long you do or don't meditate, what religious services you do or don't go to, or what prayers you do or don't say. How are any of those things going to birth a new spirit in you, or join your new spirit to me?

Everything comes as a gift from me. Your very life is a gift from me. Your next breath is a gift from me. All you can do is receive it. That is grace—what I give freely, without your behavior earning a thing. You can't earn anything by good behavior, so stop trying. At best, it's getting you nowhere. At worst, it's deceiving you into thinking you are meriting something from me. That's a lie. You're not.

You do have a vital role to play in becoming one with me, however. It is this: you must receive the gift I am offering. I don't force myself on anyone. You must, of your own free will, choose to receive what I freely offer.

There is another word for this kind of receiving. It is called *faith*. Faith is simply trust. All true, lasting relationships are built on trust. I have created you with the capacity to choose, and also the capacity to trust. The *only* way to enter into a re-

We are made right with God by placing our faith in Jesus Christ. And this is true for everyone who believes, no matter who we are. For everyone has sinned; we all fall short of God's glorious standard. Yet God, in his grace, freely makes us right in his sight. He did this through Jesus Christ when he freed us from the penalty of our sins. People are made right with God when they believe that Jesus sacrificed his life, shedding his blood. (Romans 3:22-25)

If you confess with your mouth Jesus as Lord, and believe in your heart that God raised Him from the dead, you will be saved; for with the heart a person believes, resulting in righteousness, and with the mouth he confesses, resulting in salvation. (Romans 10: 9, 10)

lationship with me, into oneness with me, is for your heart to say, "I believe that what you are saying is true. I choose to place my trust in you and everything you have done on my behalf. I choose to receive your gift."

The good news, really, is very simple. It is summed up by this:

> For God so loved the world that He gave His only begotten Son, that whoever believes [trusts] in Him should not perish, but have eternal life. (John 3:16)

To become one with me, all you have to do is place your trust in me and what I have done for you. You trust in who I am, God in the flesh. You trust that I died for your sins. And you trust that I rose from the dead on your behalf.

There are no religious rituals required to place your trust in me. We are talking about establishing a relationship, not performing rituals. Such trust can be expressed as simply as this:

> Jesus, I recognize that I need your forgiveness, and the life you offer. Thank you for dying for my sins and rising from the dead on my behalf, so that you could give me true life. I receive you by faith as my Savior and Lord. I trust you to forgive my sins, give me a new heart, join yourself to me forever, and come to live within me. Thank you for giving me new life.

It is not the words of a prayer that are vital. It is the faith that they represent.

What if your faith isn't big enough? What if you have doubts? It's not even the size of your faith that matters; what matters is the object of your faith—me. Call out to me. I will

"My sheep hear My voice, and I know them, and they follow Me; and I give eternal life to them, and they will never perish; and no one will snatch them out of My hand. My Father, who has given them to Me, is greater than all; and no one is able to snatch them out of the Father's hand." — Jesus (John 10:27-29)

hear, and respond.

When you do choose to place your trust in me, *everything* we have discussed so far becomes true for you. Your sins are forgiven. My Spirit does a heart transplant in you. The Father, Son, and Spirit come to live within you. You are forever joined to us. For the first time in your life, you begin to be what you were created to be.

You and we are one.

"I have been crucified with Christ; and it is no longer I who live, but Christ lives in me ..." *(Galatians 2:20)*

... the riches of the glory of this mystery ... which is Christ in you ... (Colossians 1:27)

In Him was life ... (John 1:4)

... all things belong to you, and you belong to Christ; and Christ belongs to God. (1 Corinthians 3:22-23)

BECAUSE WE ARE ONE, I NOW LIVE MY LIFE IN YOU

N ow we are caught up to the present. We began these lessons as if we did not know each other. You came to understand that you were created for oneness with me, the One who loves you perfectly. But your sins separated you from me. The sin issue had to be removed from between us. I took care of that on the cross. But you were also born with a rebel, sinful heart, forever at odds with me. That old heart had to be removed. I had to give you a new, righteous heart. I took care of that as well. My Spirit removed your old heart and birthed within you a new spirit. Finally, you had to be joined to me. You had to become one with me. I took care of that when you placed your trust in me. I permanently, eternally joined myself to you. I came to live in you.

You are one with me. One with the Father. One with the Spirit. And we are one with you.

So what does it mean that you are one with the God of the universe? It means everything. The entirety of your existence depends upon our oneness. You just don't understand that yet. I will show you.

What you will come to realize is that everything that follows in these lessons is *already* a reality in you. It is all yours. You don't have to work for it. You don't have to strive to get it. You can't make it true through your own efforts. It is *already* true. It is already yours. You simply experience it by faith.

Living this life operates exactly the way receiving me did in

"I am the ... life." — Jesus (John 14:6)

Therefore as you have received Christ Jesus the Lord, so walk in Him ... (Colossians 2:6)

the first place. How did you receive me? By faith. Entirely by faith. You didn't do anything to make it happen. You didn't try hard. You simply received my free gift. Receiving it is called faith. You trusted me to do it.

That's how this life operates. It doesn't work by trying hard. It doesn't work by you striving to make it happen. It works by you receiving it by faith. It all works simply by faith.

Now, here's what you will try to do. You will take all of what I am going to tell you in the rest of these lessons and try to *activate* it by your faith. If you believe hard enough, you will think, it will become true for you.

But no. Your faith doesn't activate any of what I am about to tell you. It is *already* activated. Your faith doesn't bring it into being for you. It all already is. Your faith simply acknowledges what already is.

I want you to learn to count on the things I am about to tell you. I want you to learn to live fully in them by faith. I want you to depend on me to make them a living reality in your life. I want you to put aside whatever misconceptions you have had, and embrace the simplicity of what I am saying. Embrace it, and live in its fullness. In my fullness.

This is what must finally dawn on you, then completely saturate your being:

> *It is no longer you who live. I am the One who lives in you.*

Once that awareness becomes your moment-by-moment reality, *everything* changes. And I do mean everything.

Is this a mystery? Yes. Would you expect anything less if God himself came to live in you? Would you expect it to be business as usual?

You have always thought of this life as something you

"Come to Me, all who are weary and heavy-laden, and I will give you rest. Take My yoke upon you and learn from Me ... and you will find rest for your souls. For My yoke is easy and My burden is light." (Matthew 11:28-30)

For we who have believed enter that rest ... For the one who has entered His rest has himself also rested from his works, as God did from His. (Hebrews 4:3, 10)

have to live. Before you knew me, you tried to make life work through your own effort. That works poorly. It works poorly because life was not meant to work apart from the One who is life.

But even after you came to know me, you had the same mindset about life. Life was something you had to live and make work through your own effort. Only now you were trying to do it for me. Maybe, if you asked, I would help you out from time to time. It's hard. You struggle. You fail a lot.

Of course you do! Because you are trying to do something that's impossible. You're trying to replicate my life. But there is only One who can live my life. Me.

The good news is this: I haven't asked you to replicate my life. I have come to live it in you. Living my own perfectly loving life in you is no effort for me at all.

Your life was never meant to be lived through self-effort. Your life was never meant to be about striving, self-reliance, or exercising enough self-discipline to finally get it "right." I came to deliver you from that false life, which is not really life at all. The One who is life now lives in you. I am the One who lives my perfect, always overcoming, completely sufficient life through you.

Though you are very much alive, I am actually the One living in you. I think, speak, act, and love through you. We are so connected in our one-spirit union that we *are* one, just as I and the Father are one. You and I cannot do anything other than operate as one. And in that union, I am the one living through you. Right now.

But how, as someone once asked me, can these things be? Because it sure looks like you living in you. It feels like you. Your life seems too imperfect to actually be me living it, doesn't it?

Yet this is the truth: it is no longer you who live. I am the One who lives in you. And here is where some illustrations help.

... the fullness of Him who fills all in all. (Ephesians 1:23)

... Christ is all, and in all. (Colossians 3:11)

For God, who said, "Let there be light in the darkness," has made this light shine in our hearts so we could know the glory of God that is seen in the face of Jesus Christ. We now have this light shining in our hearts, but we ourselves are like fragile clay jars containing this great treasure. This makes it clear that our great power is not from ourselves. (2 Corinthians 4:6-7)

BECAUSE WE ARE ONE, YOU ARE A CONTAINER OF ME

A lone among all creatures, I created you to be able to be joined to me. I gave you a human spirit that could become one with me. In your new birth, I gave you a new human spirit that was fully ready to receive me, and I came to live in your spirit.

That makes you a container of me. You are a vessel. You are a pot, a jar, a pitcher. You were made to contain me, and that is exactly what you do.

If I make a container, you can trust that I will fill it. That's my responsibility. I don't ask you to do it. And that is what I have done. I have filled you with myself. And having filled you with myself, my life overflows from you. You don't ever have to ask me to be with you. I am in you. You don't have to ask me to give you more of me. You are as filled with me as you can be. I live in you. I can't give you any more of myself than I have given.

This life is simple. Really. It's not about you. It's about me. You are merely the vessel. The truth about vessels is this: unless the vessel is sitting in a museum (which you aren't), the most important thing is never the vessel; it's the contents of the vessel. You want a cup of coffee. You want some tea. You want some water. It's not the cup that you're focused on. It's the coffee, the tea, or the water. *The important thing is the contents, not the vessel.*

You aren't here to be the contents of the vessel. You are

We are the temple of the living God ...
(2 Corinthians 6:16)

Do you not know that you are a temple of
God and that the Spirit of God lives in you?
(1 Corinthians 3:16)

God is love. (1 John 4:8)

here to contain Someone. That is your glory. That is your liberty. That is your fulfillment. A vessel is never able to become its contents. A cup can't become the coffee. You are the cup. I am the coffee. Stop trying to become me! Only I can be me. I never asked you to become me. I made you to be the vessel.

I want you to relax, and simply be what you are. It's easy to be a container. You contain me. I am the One living in you.

So, if you are the vessel, and I am the contents of the vessel, how much of the contents are you? None.

If you are the vessel, and I am the contents, how much of what is poured out of the vessel is you? None.

I am the everything in you. I am the all in you. You can't be the contents, only I can. You can't produce the contents. Only I can. You can't produce my life in you—any of it. Why do you think you are supposed to—or can—produce my love, my patience, my kindness, my forgiveness, my joy, my peace, my self-control? Who in the world gave you that idea? Those things don't originate with you, and they never will. You can't produce those things. Why are you trying to? Only I am those things.

Nor can I *give* you those things. You've been living with a false sense of separation. "God is up there; I am down here. I need to ask him to supply. Give me love. Give me patience. Give me self-control." *I can't give you those things.* I can't give them to you, because they don't exist apart from me.

Love is not a thing. Love is a Person. "God is love."

Love is not something that can be given. Love is a Person loving. Patience is a Person being patient. Self-control is a Person being self-controlled.

I don't give you things from heaven, so that you can live this life better. You aren't intended to live this life at all. I am the One who lives it. I live it in you.

But by His doing you are in Christ Jesus, who became to us wisdom from God, and righteousness and sanctification, and redemption ... (1 Corinthians 1:30)

Christ ... is our life ... (Colossians 3:4)

... Christ the power of God and the wisdom of God. (1 Corinthians 1:24)

That is why I am everything in you. I am the only one who can love through you, be patient through you, be self-controlled through you, be believing through you. I don't *help* you do it. I do it myself, through you. I don't give you the life. I *am* the life.

I am your wisdom. I am your power. I am your righteousness. I am your redemption. I am your sanctification. I am your everything. I am your complete sufficiency.

Does this mean you have no part to play? Of course not. You are an active cooperator in this divine process. Your role is simple, but vital: you receive it all from me. That's what containers do. If I am the All, what is left for you to be? Only a container of the All. I, the All in you, am the One living through you. You are the means by which I manifest myself—express myself—to all of the universe. Once you have that straight, life becomes easy.

Do you see how incredibly liberating this is, not having to do what you were not designed to do? Not having to be what you were not designed to be? You were designed to contain. You were designed to receive. Anyone can do that. You can do that—joyfully, peacefully, enthusiastically.

In the process, you and I enjoy a perfect union of love. A union of love that will be throughout all eternity.

"I am the vine, you are the branches; he who abides in Me and I in him, he bears much fruit, for apart from Me you can do nothing."
— *Jesus (John 15:5)*

"Do you not believe that I am in the Father, and the Father is in Me? The words that I say to you I do not speak on My own initiative, but the Father abiding in Me does His works."
— *Jesus (John 14:10)*

"As the living Father sent me, and I live because of the Father, so whoever feeds on me, he will also live because of me." — *Jesus (John 6:57)*

BECAUSE WE ARE ONE, I AM THE VINE, YOU ARE THE BRANCH

So you are a container of me. But you are not just a container. A container is lifeless, but you are not. So another illustration is helpful. I am the vine. You are the branch.

Think about a grapevine. The life comes from the vine. The branch isn't inactive. It has a role to play. But the focus is on the vine. It's the life of the vine that the branch expresses. No one, seeing wonderful grapes in a vineyard, says, "What wonderful grapes this branch produces!" No, they say, "What wonderful grapes this vine produces!" I produce. You are the expression of what I produce.

The branch is completely dependent on the vine for the life. The branch can't do anything on its own. Cut a branch off and set it on a table. How long will you have to wait for the branch to produce a grape? Forever! Branches can't produce anything.

Apart from me, you can't do anything. I live my life through you. I am the only One who can live it. It simply looks like you.

This is exactly how my Father and I operated when I was on earth. The Father lived through me, as me. I was walking between towns. I was cooking the fish. I was teaching the crowds. I was healing people. I was performing miracles. On the outside it looked like me. Except it wasn't me. I could do nothing of myself. It was the Father living in me, doing his works.

I am in the Father. He is in me. He was living His life through me, as me. There was no gap between us. There was no separation. It wasn't him living through me some of the time, and me

"Abide in Me, and I in you. As the branch cannot bear fruit of itself unless it abides in the vine, so neither can you unless you abide in Me." — Jesus (John 15:4)

... as He is, so also are we in this world. (1 John 4:17)

"I have been crucified with Christ; and it is no longer I who live, but Christ lives in me; and the life which I now live in the flesh I live by faith in the Son of God, who loved me and gave Himself up for me." (Galatians 2:20)

living through me some of the time. You operate exactly the same way. As I am, so also are you in this world.

The Father was the vine. I was the branch. Now I am the vine. You are the branch.

The key role of the branch is to receive. It receives everything from the vine. Everything the vine is, the branch receives, and simply manifests, or expresses, it. That's what you do. You manifest me. That's what you are doing right now.

Do you understand that?

This is your reality *right now*. It's not something that *becomes* a reality one day when you "get spiritual" enough. I am now the One living your ordinary, everyday life. I am handling the kids through you. I am working your job through you. I am preparing the meals through you, washing the dishes through you, living this life through you now. On the outside, it looks like you. But it's actually me doing my works through you.

I want you constantly aware of Another in you. I don't want you to see yourself as the one thinking, speaking, and acting. I want you to see me as doing those things through you, *as you*, because that's what I am doing.

Here's something I want you to grab hold of and not let go: I am pleased to live through you just as you are, *as you*.

You'll be tempted to think I'm living through you *in spite of* you—in spite of your weak humanity. No! I don't live through you in spite of your humanity, but *because* of your humanity. You're not a liability to me. You're not an impediment to my plan. You, in your humanity, are my *asset*. You're the one I've chosen to live through, just as you are, right now.

It is your weakness, your neediness, your inability, that causes my glory to shine through you. You don't have the love you need, the patience you need, the power you need to overcome. You're not meant to. So you trust that I am, right this moment,

71

And He has said to me, "My grace is sufficient for you, for power is perfected in weakness." Most gladly, therefore, I will rather boast about my weaknesses, so that the power of Christ may dwell in me. Therefore I am well content with weaknesses, with insults, with distresses, with persecutions, with difficulties, for Christ's sake; for when I am weak, then I am strong. (2 Corinthians 12:9-10)

... grow in the grace and knowledge of our Lord and Savior Jesus Christ. (2 Peter 3:18)

living my life through you. I am the love. I am the patience. I am the power. As you relax into who I am in you, you see me living through you, just as you are.

So accept yourself, just as you are. You are completely accepted by me. You are completely *acceptable* to me. I have chosen to live through your unique brand of humanness. I am perfectly pleased to be living in and through you as you are *right now*.

Stop fussing about yourself, your failures, and how you think you need to get better. I didn't call you to become better. Your job is not to become, but to contain. You're a container. Containers don't improve. Don't focus on yourself at all. Focus completely on me. I am the life in you.

I'm not calling you to recommit, rededicate, reconsecrate, or re- anything else. What would you be rededicating yourself to? Trying harder? That is what you must be delivered from!

You are the perfect means by which I express myself. If I want to express myself in different ways through you, I will make those changes. I am your sanctification, remember? Your role is to receive. You are focused on me in you, not on whatever inadequacies you think you may have.

Spiritual growth is not about improving yourself so that your weaknesses disappear. I use your weaknesses to my glory. Spiritual growth is about *receiving*. The Holy Spirit has come to show you the things you are *freely given*.

Here's what I want you to grow in. Grow in the *grace* and *knowledge* of me. Grace means I give, you receive. Grow in your receiving of me as the One who is living in you each moment. And the knowledge of me as what? As the One who lives in you, through you, as you.

I am the vine. You are the branch. I flow through you. This entire life is lived by grace, by receiving, from faith to faith— one episode of faith in me living in you to the next.

But as many as received Him, to them He gave the right to become children of God, even to those who believe in His name ... (John 1:12)

For of His fullness we have all received, and grace upon grace. (John 1:16)

"Truly I say to you, whoever does not receive the kingdom of God like a child will not enter it at all." — Jesus (Mark 10:15)

BECAUSE WE ARE ONE, YOU SIMPLY RECEIVE BY FAITH

One time I stood a little child before my disciples and said to them, "Whoever humbles himself like this child is the greatest in the kingdom of heaven."

Why? Because with children, everything must be simple. Children are humble. They simply receive. It's pretty much all they do. And they are perfectly happy doing it.

That's what you are designed to do. Be like a child. Just receive.

All of life involves receiving. In the natural realm, plants receive energy from the sun, water from the sky, and nourishment from the soil. Animals receive the food I provide them. You receive the air you breathe, the water you drink, the food you eat. All of creation functions by receptivity.

The same applies in the spiritual realm. You simply receive. Receptivity is the most child-like function you can have, and the most natural. It is not *one* of your functions. It *is* your function. All of your other functions are by-products of this one. Children are wonderful receivers. You are my Father's child, remember?

When you receive, your focus is on what is being received. If you are being thrown a baseball, your focus isn't on the perfection of your glove; it's on the baseball coming at you (or, at least, it needs to be!). If you are sitting down to eat, your focus isn't on the complexity of your digestive system. It's on the food you are receiving.

The righteous shall live by faith. (Romans 1:17)

The righteous shall live by faith. (Galatians 3:11)

The righteous shall live by faith. (Hebrews 10:38)

Therefore as you have received Christ Jesus the Lord, so walk in Him ... (Colossians 2:6)

Because we are one, it's not your activity that is key in our union. It's your receptivity. That's how I live my life through you, through your receptivity. That's how we entered into a one-spirit union in the first place. You received me. That is still your role, to receive.

What is it, then, that you receive? Do you receive my help? No, I didn't come to help you live the life. I came to live it in you. Do you receive the love, the patience, the power? No, I don't have those *things* to give you. I only have myself to give you. And that is exactly what you receive. You receive me, living my life in you, and through you. I am already in you, living through you. I simply want you to receive more fully the reality of me living in you.

And how, you may ask, do you receive? By faith.

Remember what the Bible's word for receptivity is? *Faith*. It is not striving hard after anything. It's simply receiving what already is. In truth, it is simply *recognizing* what already is. What already is, is me, living my life in you and through you. You simply accept that as the present-tense reality. It doesn't *become* the reality when you believe hard enough. It is the reality. Right now.

All of life is lived by faith, even in the physical realm. You are invited to someone's home. You are given an address. You've never been there. You don't even know if there is a house at that address. But you have faith that what your hosts have told you is true. So you go in faith, trusting that when you arrive, a house will be there.

Once there, you go in. Everyone is invited to have a seat. You spot a wooden chair. You have no idea if the chair will hold you. You've never sat in it before. But you trust that your hosts won't put a chair out that is going to collapse. By faith, you sit. Dinner is served. You've never eaten anything at this home before ...

... the life which I now live in the flesh I live by the faith of the Son of God, who loved me, and gave himself for me. (Galatians 2:20b)

... fixing our eyes on Jesus, the author and perfecter of faith ... (Hebrews 12:2)

Do you see? You are operating entirely on faith in someone, and what that someone has told you. Your faith doesn't create the reality. The house was already there. The chair that would hold you was already there. Through faith you simply recognized the reality that already was. You could have said, "I don't believe that chair will hold me," and walked out.

It is no different in the spiritual realm. Faith doesn't create the reality. Faith is simply recognizing what is already there. It is continually recognizing the life of Another in you. You trust in me, and what I tell you: I am in you; you are in me; I am living my life through you. I am speaking, acting, loving through you. It is no longer you who live. It is me living through you, expressing all that I am through you.

You relax into this reality. That is your divinely-ordained role. You are the container. You are the one trusting me, depending on me each moment to make it a reality. Ours is a union in which I produce the fruit, and you manifest it. You can't produce it. But you allow it to be expressed through you. That happens through faith.

But that's too simple, you may object. Yes, it is simple. I told you that this life is simple. It has to be if you are to receive it like a child. I am inviting you to enter my rest, in the here and now. How else are you going to be at rest other than by simply receiving?

The wonderful thing is that you don't even have to work up this faith that I am the one living in you. *You live by my faith.* I am the Believer in you. You lean on me to have sufficient faith. You depend on me for your faith, just as you depend on me for everything else. I am your faith. I am the One living in you, and through you. Right now.

Now we have received, not the spirit of the world, but the Spirit who is from God, so that we may know the things freely given to us by God ... (1 Corinthians 2:12)

But when He, the Spirit of truth, comes, He will guide you into all the truth ... He will glorify Me, for He will take of Mine and will disclose it to you. (John 16:13-14)

But having the same spirit of faith, according to what is written, "I believed, therefore I spoke," we also believe, therefore we also speak ... (2 Corinthians 4:13)

LESSON 10

BECAUSE WE ARE ONE, MY SPIRIT MAKES YOU KNOW

E ventually, the faith you are exercising dissolves into simply *knowing*. That's the work of the Holy Spirit. His primary task in you is to reveal me to you. And where is he going to reveal me? *In you*, because that's where I live. The Spirit comes that you might *know* the things that God has freely given you. And what, primarily, have you been freely given? Me! Me living in you.

This is how God's work is done in you. God freely gives. The Spirit reveals it to you. You choose to trust in what you've been shown. And eventually, by the Spirit's work in you, your choice to trust dissolves into knowing. At that point faith becomes substance. It becomes evidence. It is as real to you as things in the physical world.

You experience this process all the time in the material world. Take the example from earlier. You are invited to sit in a chair you've never sat in before. You don't know if it will hold you or not. But you trust that it will, and you sit. At that point, you know. You don't have to keep affirming it. You simply know.

But your knowing didn't come by you standing in front of the chair and trying to work up knowing. The knowing wasn't produced by you at all. The chair itself produced the knowing. What you trusted in produced the knowing.

You've experienced this before in the spiritual realm as well. At some point (whether you know when that time was or not), you placed your trust in me and received the new birth from the Spirit. At that point you trusted that your sins were forgiv-

*Now faith is the substance of things hoped for,
the evidence of things not seen. (Hebrews 11:1)*

*... we have received grace and apostleship to
bring about the obedience of faith among all the
Gentiles for His name's sake. (Romans 1:5)*

*... while we look not at the things which are
seen, but at the things which are not seen;
for the things which are seen are temporal,
but the things which are not seen are eternal.
(2 Corinthians 4:18)*

en. Eventually (and it may have been very quickly), that trust became knowing. You didn't have to keep reminding yourself that your sins were forgiven. You simply knew.

Putting your faith in *me in you* operates the same way. Once upon a time you heard the word, "Jesus can save you." And you may have thought, "Jesus can save *me*? No way." But eventually you chose to trust. And you discovered it was true. Now I am telling you that I am in you, living my life through you. And you look at your own life and think, "Jesus is living through me? Look at all my failures! No way."

You enter in by faith. That's the obedience I'm looking for—not you trying your hardest to live like me, but rather the obedience of faith: you believing and affirming what I tell you.

Boldly grasp hold of me by faith. Declare by faith that we are one, that it is indeed me living my life in you and through you. As you do, you will enter into what *already is*. You will be strong, for I am the strength in you. You will be loving, for I am love within you. You will be wise, for I am wisdom within you. You will have joy, peace, self-control, and every other fruit of the Spirit, for I am all of those things in you.

Declare it by faith, and keep declaring it. As you confess it with your mouth, you will begin to experience the reality of it. But your confession doesn't make it a reality. It simply enables you to fully enter into what already is. I am the One living through you. Your job is to affirm. Your job isn't to work up the knowing. Only my Spirit can produce the knowing. You affirm. He confirms. That's His job.

As you affirm, often *despite* external appearances to the contrary, faith finally becomes fact in you. My Spirit causes your affirming to become a settled awareness. You simply know. At that point you are living completely spontaneously. You know that it's actually me living through you. Because it is. It always has been.

"This is My commandment, that you love one another, just as I have loved you. Greater love has no one than this, that one lay down his life for his friends." — Jesus (John 15:12-13)

"For even the Son of Man did not come to be served, but to serve, and to give His life a ransom for many." (Mark 10:45)

We know love by this, that He laid down His life for us; and we ought to lay down our lives for the brethren. (1 John 3:16)

Beloved, let us love one another, for love is from God; and everyone who loves is born of God and knows God. (1 John 4:7)

BECAUSE WE ARE ONE, I LIVE MY LIFE OF OTHER-LOVE THROUGH YOU

I f we are one, and I am now the One living through you, what is the nature of this life I am living in you? There are only two choices: a self-seeker or a self-giver; a self-lover or an other-lover. I am eternally an other-lover. I am a self-giver. Everything I do, I do for the benefit, the welfare, of the other.

"God so loved the world that He *gave* ..."

"I am the good shepherd; the good shepherd lays down his life for the sheep."

That is what I did for you. And that is what I will do *through* you. I will always be a self-giver, an other-lover, through you.

This can seem hard. Everything in this world screams that the way to fulfillment is to be a self-lover, a self-seeker. You have to grab what you can out of this world. It's a lie. It doesn't lead to fulfillment. You can see that it's a lie by simply looking around you. But lies are deceptively appealing.

If you are born of God and joined to me, you have forever died to being a self-getter. You share in my nature, and your true nature is mine: to be an other-lover. You have the privilege of allowing me to lay down my life through you for others. That means your life being laid down as well.

The gratifications that the world offers are obvious and often immediate. They are also short-lived. What may not be immediately apparent, but becomes very clear in experience, is the utter fulfillment in being for others. I am the infinitely

"I am the bread of life; he who comes to Me will not hunger, and he who believes in Me will never thirst." — Jesus (John 6:35)

Do nothing from selfishness or empty conceit, but with humility of mind regard one another as more important than yourselves. (Philippians 2:3)

But we have this treasure in clay jars, so that the extraordinary power belongs to God and does not come from us. We are ... always carrying around in our body the death of Jesus, so that the life of Jesus may also be made visible in our body. For we who are alive are constantly being handed over to death for Jesus' sake, so that the life of Jesus may also be made visible in our mortal body. As a result, death is at work in us, but life is at work in you. (2 Corinthians 4:7, 10-12)

happy God; I am completely self-giving.

How can you be free to be a self-giver, to allow me to love others through you, to always seek what is best for the other person? It is only possible as you take the faith step of affirming that I am your fulfillment. I meet all of your inner needs. I am the living water that has quenched your thirst. As you continually take that faith step, my Spirit makes it a reality in your experience. Faith dissolves into knowing. You *know* that I am your fulfillment. You are freed from having to constantly seek to get from others—seek to get what they cannot give you. How is a limited, finite world—how are limited, finite beings—ever going to be your fulfillment? You were created for the divine. You were created for the infinite.

I am your fulfillment. Right now. You *are* full on the inside, and the rivers of living water flow out from you to others.

As with everything else, however, this is a faith process. You hear what I say, you grab it by faith despite appearances to the contrary, and you affirm it, over and over. My Spirit confirms it in you, and you become a knower.

In love, I have joined you to myself forever. You are now my means of bringing life to others. They are thirsty. They will see my life in you and be drawn to it. They will see your peace, your joy, the other-love flowing through you in the midst of difficult circumstances. It will look like you, but you know it's me in you. You know that you're simply the container.

Clay jars are meant to be used. You are the means by which my other-giving love is shown to the world. In the process, you are filled. Being poured out for others becomes your joy. You share in the abundant life of the infinitely happy God.

But if you are to be fully available as my vessel, through which I live my other-love life, you need something—something that actually you already have. You need my mind. You need to see as I see.

... But we have the mind of Christ. (1 Corinthians 2:16)

For from Him and through Him and to Him are all things. (Romans 11:36)

[God] works all things after the counsel of His will. (Ephesians 1:11)

BECAUSE WE ARE ONE, YOU SEE ME IN EVERYTHING

You live in a world that, because of sin, is not as it one day will be. It's messed up. Nothing is quite right. Life is an endless stream of circumstances that range from annoying to heartbreaking. I know. I live in this world in you, as you. The question is this: how are you going to choose to see these circumstances—as the world does, or as I do? Because we are one, you can see as I do. In fact, you have the very mind of Christ.

I don't just see the appearance of things. What I see is reality. And the reality is this: I am in everything. I want you to see me in everything.

I am in everything for your good, and the good of others. The beautiful sunset? I am in that. The cute kids selling lemonade on the corner? I am in that. The flat tire you discovered this morning when you walked out of the house? I am in that. The bad grades your child has in math? I am in that. The difficult news you just got from the doctor? I am in that.

I am in *everything*. I am not standing idly by, hoping for the best. I am in it for good. Does that mean I caused it? I'm not talking about cause, and I don't want you to be focused on cause. It's a complete distraction. I want you to understand that you have a God who is bigger than the decisions of people, bigger than the works of the devil, bigger than any heartbreak of life, and that I am not only in it for good, I mean it for good. Yes, if you are in a circumstance, I mean that circumstance

So Jesus said to Peter, "Put the sword into the sheath; the cup which the Father has given Me, shall I not drink it?" (John 18:11)

And we know that God causes all things to work together for good to those who love God, to those who are called according to His purpose. For those whom He foreknew, He also predestined to become conformed to the image of His Son, so that He would be the firstborn among many brethren. (Romans 8:28-29)

But in all these things we overwhelmingly conquer through Him who loved us. For I am convinced that neither death, nor life, nor angels, nor principalities, nor things present, nor things to come, nor powers, nor height, nor depth, nor any other created thing, will be able to separate us from the love of God, which is in Christ Jesus our Lord. (Romans 8:37-39)

for good. The universe is completely safe for you. Nothing comes to you—nothing comes to me in you—unless it passes through my loving hands.

This is where you see with the eyes of faith. Because every circumstance doesn't appear good. Some appear horrible. Some appear downright evil. How do you think the cross looked to me? But do you remember what I told my disciples it was? "This is my Father's cup for me," I told them. It wasn't the religious leaders' cup for me. It wasn't the Romans' cup for me. It wasn't the devil's cup for me. It was my Father's cup. And out of that evil he brought the redemption of the world.

I am doing that through you. I am taking you into difficult circumstances. You don't like them. You wouldn't choose them. That's perfectly normal. No one likes difficulty. But you choose to see me in it for good. You say, "Lord, despite appearances, you mean this for good."

And as you do, you see my Spirit at work, working it for good. It may not be right away. It may even be something that *you* never physically see. But you see it now by faith, and you will see it in eternity. You choose to stop focusing on the negative, and instead see my perfection in the situation.

Sometimes the circumstances are for teaching you. How are you going to learn that I, living in you, through you, am your sufficiency, unless a circumstance arises that threatens insufficiency? You see your lack, so you are driven to me. You learn to relax into the One who, in you, is completely sufficient. You learn peace and rest, even in the midst of chaos.

Or how are you going to learn that I am your deliverer, unless you are in a situation that causes you to turn to me, that I may deliver you?

Often the circumstances have little to do with my program *in* you at all; they have to do with my program *through* you. You

"As for you, you meant evil against me, but God meant it for good in order to bring about this present result, to preserve many people alive." — Joseph (Genesis 50:20)

For we walk by faith, not by sight. (2 Corinthians 5:7)

Consider it all joy, my brethren, when you encounter various trials, knowing that the testing of your faith produces endurance. And let endurance have its perfect result, so that you may be perfect and complete, lacking in nothing. (James 1:2-4)

are taken through a hardship. You are taken through a deep heartache. Why, you wonder, doesn't God take this away?

But you and I are one. And two things are true. First, I am your fulfillment, even in the midst of hardship and heartache. You learn that—you experience that—as you walk through in faith. Second, your trials make you a vessel prepared to show my love to those going through the same trials. How are you going to truly relate to people unless you have walked in their shoes? How are you going to show them my love, and my sufficiency, unless you've experienced my sufficiency in ways that apply to their situation?

This is where you and I are one in laying down our lives for others. It's where you share in my sufferings for a broken world. You say, "Lord, I don't see the point of this trial. It feels terrible. But you mean it for good, and you are in it for someone's good. I receive that and trust you as my sufficiency." Then you see me living my life through you, manifesting my life to those who need me.

You could call this kind of seeing the *single eye*. It's not seeing the apparent evil or bad as the ultimate reality. It's only seeing me in everything. It's only seeing me in yourself. I am the One living through you. It's only seeing me in others. I am the One living through them, or at work in them, or using them as my instruments to bring about my good purposes. It's only seeing me in your circumstance. By faith you know that I mean it for good, and I am in it for good.

Don't see "God and." See "God only"—in yourself, in others, in your circumstances. I am all you see. And seeing by faith, you are ready to be my vessel for good in that very situation. My life comes pouring out through you as you take your faith stand. Now you and I are being poured out for the world together. And as we are, you are being filled with my rivers of living water.

Therefore if anyone is in Christ, he is a new creature; the old things passed away; behold, new things have come. Now all things are from God ... (2 Corinthians 5:17-18)

Knowing this, that our old self was crucified with Him ... (Romans 6:6)

"I have been crucified with Christ ..." (Galatians 2:20)

BECAUSE WE ARE ONE, YOU ARE A RIGHTEOUS NEW CREATION

So far, these lessons have focused on the reality of us being one, of me living in you, through you, as you. Having spent time discussing that reality, I want to turn to some issues that it's easy to be confused about, but which are vital for you to understand. The truth of our being one will clarify most of these.

The first reality is this: when you placed your faith in me, you became a *completely* new person. The old person that you were *ceased to exist.* You are now a righteous new creation.

How is that possible? This is how.

There are mysteries in the realm of spirit that will never be apparent to the natural eye. My living in you is one of them. To the natural eye, it looks like you are living in you, not me. Just as, two thousand years ago, it looked like I was living in me on earth, not the Father.

In the same way, at the cross, much happened in the realm of spirit that you can only accept by faith. I tell you it is true, and you can only affirm it. As you do, your life will bear witness to it.

One significant thing that happened at the cross is that your sins were forgiven. Nothing in the material realm tells you that. It is a spirit reality. You receive me by faith, and my Spirit and the Scriptures confirm to you that, at the cross, all of your sins were forgiven. You live based on that spirit reality.

Something else vital happened on the cross as well. Your old man—your old, independent spirit, at war with me—was

For the love of Christ controls us, having concluded this, that one died for all, therefore all died ... (2 Corinthians 5:14)

He made Him who knew no sin to be sin on our behalf, so that we might become the righteousness of God in Him. (2 Corinthians 5:21)

The new self ... in the likeness of God has been created in righteousness and holiness of the truth. (Ephesians 4:24)

crucified with me. This death wasn't something metaphorical, as if you are simply to think of yourself as leaving the old life behind. It actually happened. It was as real as my own death. In the same way I was crucified on the cross, your old man was crucified there. When I died on the cross, your old man died as well.

How did this happen? Because we are one spirit, what happens to me, happens to you. You are joined to me. And because God exists outside of time, your union with me exists outside of time. That's why you are chosen in me before the foundation of the world. That's why I am the Lamb slain for you from before the foundation of the world. And that's why, being one with me, when I went to the cross, you went to the cross, and there your old man died.

I didn't stay in the grave after I was crucified, and because you are one with me, neither did you. When I was raised from the dead, you were raised with me. Only, it wasn't your old man who was raised. It was your new man, "created in righteousness and holiness of the truth."

This is the heart transplant I promised the Hebrews would become a reality one day, the new birth in you from my Spirit. I take out your heart of stone; I give you a new heart. It's all describing the same thing. The old you died and was taken out. The new you was born of my Spirit. You were raised with me. You were made alive with me.

Who you were in the depths of your being *had* to change. I couldn't join myself to your old man—your old, rebellious, sinful spirit that you were humanly born with. Have you read who the Scriptures say your old man was? You were:

> dead in your trespasses and sins, conducting
> your life according to the way of the world,

As those who have been chosen of God, holy and beloved ... (Colossians 3:12)

... in Him you have been made complete ... (Colossians 2:10)

living in the lusts of your flesh, indulging the lusts of the flesh and of the mind. You were darkened in your understanding, having a futile mind, excluded from my life because of the ignorance that was in you, because of the hardness of your heart. You were darkness, a son or daughter of the night, a son or daughter of disobedience. You didn't know me and were separated from me. You were disobedient, deceived, enslaved to various lusts and pleasures, spending your life in malice and envy, hateful, hating one another. You were ungodly, unrighteous, unclean, a slave of sin. You were my enemy.

How could I eternally join myself to that person? It was impossible. So I took that person to the cross with me. He died. He no longer exists. When I rose from the dead, I raised a completely new person, a new man, in his place. This new person is a:

> partaker of the divine nature, a saint, light in the Lord, a son or daughter of light, the righteousness of God, holy, blameless, made complete, perfected for all time, a slave of righteousness, sanctified, glorified, washed, created in righteousness and holiness, my own possession, alive to God, a fragrance of me to God, a fellow heir with me, God's elect, redeemed, God's child, my friend, God's temple, reconciled to God, a partaker of me, chosen, dearly loved, a fellow citizen of heaven with all of God's saints, joined to me, one spirit with me, a part of my body, born of God.

But as many as received Him, to them He gave the right to become children of God, even to those who believe in His name, who were born, not of blood nor of the will of the flesh nor of the will of man, but of God. (John 1:12-13)

For by one offering He has perfected for all time those who are being sanctified. (Hebrews 10:14)

Do you see? Your identity didn't just change "positionally." I don't just pretend you are a new person. In the depths of your being, you *are* a completely new person. The old sinner ceased to exist. A new, righteous saint was raised in his place. You are a completely new creation. "The old has passed away; the new has come." Now, in you, "*all* things are from God."

So why do you still sin? We will get to that. But first, I want you to fully embrace who you are in me. Stop thinking of yourself as a sinner. You aren't. Stop calling yourself a sinner. You're not. You're a saint, a holy one.

Nor are you part saint, part sinner, as if there are two of "you," fighting it out. You aren't still part old man. *I couldn't have joined myself to you if you were!* Your old man was killed on the cross. You are the new man. You are born of my Spirit. You are born of God. God doesn't give birth to part-sinner, part-saint. You *are* the righteousness of God. You are *completely* acceptable. I made you that way.

You are a righteous new creation. In the depths of your heart, you are one hundred percent on my side. That's who I became one spirit with. Fully embrace who you are. I have. And having embraced who you now are, I joined myself to you, forever.

... but now once at the consummation of the ages He has been manifested to put away sin by the sacrifice of Himself. (Hebrews 9:26)

There is therefore now no condemnation for those who are in Christ Jesus. (Romans 8:1)

Who will bring a charge against God's elect? God is the one who justifies; who is the one who condemns? Christ Jesus is He who died, yes, rather who was raised, who is at the right hand of God, who also intercedes for us. (Romans 8:33-34)

I am writing to you, little children, because your sins have been forgiven you for His name's sake. (1 John 2:12)

BECAUSE WE ARE ONE, THE SIN ISSUE BETWEEN US IS GONE

So the first reality when you trusted in me is that you became an entirely new person. The old person that you were no longer exists. You are now a righteous new creation.

The second reality is this: I have completely taken the sin issue between us off the table. It is gone. I came to completely take away the sin issue at the cross, and I completely took it away!

What does this mean for you? For one, it means that there is never, ever any condemnation for you. Do you understand why there *can't* be any condemnation for you? You and I are one. What happens to me happens to you. What happens to you happens to me. If you are condemned, I am condemned.

I paid the penalty for every one of your sins, past, present, and future. If the Father were to condemn you for anything, he would be saying to me, "Your death was insufficient. The penalty you paid wasn't enough." Do you think he is going to do that?

Besides, who is there left to condemn? Your old man, the source of your sins, has already been executed on the cross with me. The only "you" who exists now is the new man, birthed by my Spirit. You are born of God. On what basis would the Father condemn your holy, righteous new man?

There is no condemnation for those who are in me. So don't take any condemnation—from the devil, from others, or from accusing thoughts that are never from me. I want you living in

When you were dead in your transgressions and the uncircumcision of your flesh, He made you alive together with Him, having forgiven us all our transgressions, having canceled out the certificate of debt consisting of decrees against us, which was hostile to us, and He has taken it out of the way, having nailed it to the cross. (Colossians 2:13)

Just as David also speaks of the blessing on the man to whom God credits righteousness apart from works: "Blessed are those whose lawless deeds have been forgiven, and whose sins have been covered. Blessed is the man whose sin the Lord will not take into account." (Romans 4:6-8)

God is educating you; that's why you must never drop out. He's treating you as dear children. This trouble you're in isn't punishment; it's training, the normal experience of children. (Hebrews 12:7)

BECAUSE WE ARE ONE, THE SIN ISSUE BETWEEN US IS GONE

the extravagant freedom of my full forgiveness. Because you are fully forgiven.

Reject as well any general sense of condemnation. "You're not good enough. You don't measure up. You keep falling into the same sins." That *never* comes from me. You are the one I have chosen to live through, just as you are. You are not a liability to me. You are my asset. You are my chosen vessel. I am *pleased* to live my life through you.

You and I are one. You are not just accepted; you are completely acceptable.

Not only are you not condemned for any sin you commit, *the Father doesn't even deal with you according to your sins.* The Father only deals with you out of his tender love for you, according to what is best for you. He no longer takes your sins into account.

But what about God's discipline, you ask. You fear that God will punish you—discipline you—for your sins.

No. Absolutely not. I dealt with the sin issue at the cross, both for the here and now and for eternity. It is off the table, remember? You and I are one. Is the Father going to discipline me for your sins as well? "Blessed is the man whose sin the Lord will not take into account." That is you!

So what is discipline? Discipline simply means *training.* Because I have removed the sin issue, the training doesn't involve accounting for your sins. Instead, the training is the process of growing you up. It is the process of me being fully formed in you. That's what I'm after. I am fully formed in you when I am living my life in its fullness through you. Sometimes that process involves failure, pain, and hardship. You must learn that the way of self-effort, even religious self-effort, is not my life. Your self-effort has to fail before you are ready to embrace me as your life.

So training can at times be difficult. But you have nothing

There is no fear in love; but perfect love casts out fear ... (1 John 4:18)

My children, with whom I am again in labor until Christ is formed in you ... (Galatians 4:19)

For the Law, since it has only a shadow of the good things to come and not the very form of things, can never, by the same sacrifices which they offer continually year by year, make perfect those who draw near. Otherwise, would they not have ceased to be offered, because the worshipers, having once been cleansed, would no longer have had consciousness of sins? ... but [Jesus], having offered one sacrifice for sins for all time, sat down at the right hand of God ... For by one offering He has perfected for all time those who are sanctified. (Hebrews 10:1-2, 12, 14)

to fear from it. Perfect love casts out all fear, and I love you perfectly. I never do anything toward you that is not for your very best. How could I? We are one.

Far from dealing with you according to your sins, I came to do just the opposite in you. I came to deliver you from sin-consciousness. I don't want you looking for sin in your life. I don't want you focused on avoiding sin, either. You already died to it. It has no power over you. I don't want you focused on sin, period. I forgave all your sins. I crucified your old man, who was the source of sin in you. I already dealt with sin!

Don't you see that having a sin-consciousness is completely contrary to me living my life in you? As long as you are focused on sin, you aren't focused on me. And when you are focused on sin instead of me, you fall back into self-effort and self-improvement. "I have to get my act together for God!"

No. Just … no. That's a dead end. I want your focus entirely on me. I am the life in you. I am everything in you. I live in you, and I *always* live unto the Father. Only I can do that.

Be conscious of me. Period. Have a Christ-consciousness, not a sin-consciousness. And if you do something that clearly doesn't originate with me, simply agree with the Holy Spirit about it. "Lord, that wasn't of you." Then look back at me in faith. Affirm that I am living my life through you, regardless of how it appears. Affirm that I am doing that in you right now. Affirm it over and over, and I will show in you, and through you, that it is true.

The one who joins himself to the Lord is one spirit with Him. (1 Corinthians 6:17)

"In that day you will know that I am in My Father, and you in Me, and I in you."
— Jesus (John 14:20)

For I am convinced that neither death, nor life, nor angels, nor principalities, nor things present, nor things to come, nor powers, nor height, nor depth, nor any other created thing, will be able to separate us from the love of God, which is in Christ Jesus our Lord. (Romans 8:38-39)

BECAUSE WE ARE ONE, THERE IS NEVER ANY SEPARATION BETWEEN US

I have completely taken care of the sin issue at the cross. But by reflex you imagine that your sins change your relationship with me. Your sins separate you from me, you think. They take you out of fellowship with me. As long as you don't confess them, you remain out of fellowship with me.

No. None of that is true. Those beliefs keep you in bondage. They keep you sin-conscious. I came to set you free from all that.

Here's why these things are untrue. You and I are one. Permanently, eternally one. You have become one spirit with me. That's as close as we can possibly get. In all the ages to come, you won't be any closer than one spirit with me. You will experience more fully the reality of that closeness, but you won't get any closer. There can never again be any separation between us. There can never again be any distance between us. Since you are in me, you are now and always will be as close to the Father as I am. That's how close I have brought you.

Nothing you do can produce any separation between us. I will repeat that. *Nothing you do can produce any separation between us.* That includes taking you out of fellowship with me. Fellowship simply means *to share, to participate in together.* You share in my life. You are a partaker of my nature. Does committing a sin take my life away from you? Do I stop being in you if you sin? Do you stop being a partaker of my nature? No!

Our fellowship is with the Father, and with His Son Jesus Christ. (1 John 1:3)

I am writing to you, little children, because your sins have been forgiven you for His name's sake. (1 John 2:12)

When you were dead in your transgressions and the uncircumcision of your flesh, He made you alive together with Him, having forgiven us all our transgressions. (Colossians 2:13)

He made Him who knew no sin to be sin on our behalf, so that we might become the righteousness of God in Him. (2 Corinthians 5:21)

The truth is this: you committing a sin doesn't move you one inch from me. It can't. We are one spirit. That never changes. You share in my life. That never changes. You are not constantly hopping in and out of fellowship with me.

What your sin does is affect your enjoyment, your experience, of our oneness. But it doesn't move you away from me. That's a huge difference. Your fellowship, your sharing, your participation, is still with me, and with the Father, and with the Spirit. You can be at complete rest in your oneness with me. Nothing ever separates us. Nothing.

If sinning doesn't take you *out* of fellowship with me, then confessing your sin cannot bring you back *into* fellowship with me. Nor does confessing your sin activate your forgiveness. Your forgiveness was already activated, and completed, once and for all time, at the cross. You don't have to do anything to get forgiven. If you did, that would mean you needed to add to my work on the cross. But you don't. You are already completely forgiven.

So should you agree with my Spirit if he points out that you have sinned? Absolutely. But it's not to get forgiven, or to be restored to any lost fellowship. It's simply so that you will be on the same page as me. It's so you're saying what I say about something you said or did, that it didn't originate from me, and thanking me that you are already completely forgiven, and trusting once again in my sufficiency to live through you.

I have made you as close to myself as you can ever be. Nothing can change that. And nothing can change the fact that I am the life within you. Do you want to know the confession that really pleases me? Confess that you are the righteousness of God. Confess that I am the one living in you, and through you. That's the consistent confession that will bear fruit in your life.

… knowing this, that our old self was crucified with Him, in order that our body of sin might be made powerless, so that we would no longer be slaves to sin; for he who has died is freed from sin. (Romans 6:6-7)

… How shall we who died to sin still live in it? (Romans 6:2)

For I joyfully concur with the law of God in the inner man … (Romans 7:22)

For the death that He died, He died to sin once for all; but the life that He lives, He lives to God. (Romans 6:10)

BECAUSE WE ARE ONE, SIN IS POWERLESS OVER YOU

N ow, to the issue of sin's power over you. It doesn't have any.

I know, that doesn't seem to be true. Your feelings tell you it's not true. Your experience screams at you it's not true.

I'm telling you it's true. Who are you going to believe?

When your old man died at the cross, you died to sin. You don't feel freed from the power of sin. You don't look freed from the power of sin. You may not act freed from the power of sin. But you *have been* freed from the power of sin.

The old man was the source of sin within you. From it, all sins flowed. The power of sin resided in it. And when your old man died, guess what? The union of your spirit to sin was forever severed. You were freed from sin's grasp. You were freed from its power. It no longer has any claim on you.

I, too, died to sin on the cross. Not that it ever had a rightful claim on me, but at the cross I chose to *become* sin on your behalf. I fully submitted to its every claim. But when I died, I died to it. And since you are one with me, you died to it. It no longer has a claim on either of us.

When I was raised, I was raised alive to God. You, too, were raised alive to God. The life that we live together, we live to the Father. Sin has no claim on us. Sin has no power over us. You are no longer a container of sin. You are a container of me.

So why can you still sin? Because you live in an unredeemed body. The power of sin still resides in your physical members.

So now, no longer am I the one doing it, but sin which dwells in me … For the good that I want, I do not do, but I practice the very evil that I do not want. But if I am doing the very thing I do not want, I am no longer the one doing it, but sin which dwells in me. (Romans 7:17, 19, 20)

… but I see a different law in the members of my body, waging war against the law of my mind and making me a prisoner of the law of sin which is in my members. Wretched man that I am! Who will set me free from the body of this death? Thanks be to God through Jesus Christ our Lord! (Romans 7:23-25)

For the law of the Spirit of life in Christ Jesus has set you free from the law of sin and of death. (Romans 8:2)

But thanks be to God, who always leads us in triumph in Christ … (2 Corinthians 2:14)

Your body was born with a sinful spirit and from birth was trained to sin. So sin can call to you from your body. One day, you will eject from it, and sin will no longer even call to you.

But those calls, however strong they may feel, are not who you are. Your old man, your sinful spirit, was crucified. He was removed. You received a new heart, born of my Spirit. You are holy and righteous. Your heart is for me. Despite feelings to the contrary, there is no one in the depths of your being who *wants* to sin. So if you do heed those calls and do choose to sin, it's not the real you who is sinning. It is sin still hanging out in your bodily members. I see the difference. I know where your heart is. I know you are simply being deceived.

This isn't an excuse to sin. It's a recognition of reality. You died to sin. Affirm that. Say it repeatedly. Even sin that remains in your bodily members has been rendered powerless. Its hold on you has been broken, because its hold on me was broken. I *only* live to the Father. I only live to the Father through you.

Struggling in your self-effort against sin is useless. Why? Because sin, at its heart, is not just bad deeds. It is living for self. It is the spirit of unlove, not other-love. So self-effort is useless against it. Self-effort is Satan's principle for living. It is trying to live independently of me. Living-for-self is *empowered* by self-effort, not defeated by it. A life of self-struggle against sin leads nowhere but self-condemnation.

The key to dealing with sin's deceitful calls is the same as the key to everything else. You and I are one. It is no longer you who live. I live in you, and I always live to the Father. I will live my completely overcoming, always victorious, perfectly loving life to the Father through you, as you. You affirm that. You relax into that. And as you do, my Spirit will confirm it in you. You will enter into—by experience—what is already fact: sin has no power over you. I am the victory in you, through you.

115

[You] were made to die to the Law through the body of Christ, so that you might be joined to another, to Him who was raised from the dead, in order that we might bear fruit for God. For while we were in the flesh, the sinful passions, which were aroused by the Law, were at work in the members of our body to bear fruit for death. But now we have been released from the Law, having died to that by which we were bound, so that we serve in newness of the Spirit and not in oldness of the letter. (Romans 7:4-6)

For as many as are of the works of the Law are under a curse; for it is written, "Cursed is everyone who does not abide by all things written in the book of the law, to perform them." ... the Law is not of faith; on the contrary, "He who practices them shall live by them." Christ redeemed us from the curse of the Law, having become a curse for us ... (Galatians 3:10-13)

... the power of sin is the law. (1 Corinthians 15:56)

BECAUSE WE ARE ONE, YOU NO LONGER LIVE BY RULES

I t isn't just sin that no longer has any power over you. You died to something else on the cross, too. You died to living according to rules.

I know, this is counter-intuitive. How could you possibly no longer live by rules? Isn't that just a license to sin?

No, it's actually a license to live exactly the way I designed you to live. Let me explain why.

I have come to live in you. I am now the life in you. I am the One living this life through you. And who am I? The eternal, all-powerful, all-sufficient, all-loving God.

Do you think I need laws to behave myself? Do I need rules to keep me in line? Of course not! I myself am the fulfillment of the entire law, the law of love. I forever live my life of perfect other-love. I live it in you. I live it through you. I do it effortlessly. It is who I am.

Now let's hypothetically put you back under various laws and rules that you think you have to keep. What has just happened? Your focus has immediately left me. Your focus is no longer on the One living through you. It's now on the laws that you are supposed to keep. And where does that take you? Back into self-effort! You are now trying your best to keep the rules that you've been given. And where does self-effort lead you? Into defeat, because you were never meant to live this life on your own. Self-reliance doesn't work. The law doesn't keep you from sin. It actually *empowers* sin.

Therefore the Law has become our tutor to lead us to Christ, so that we may be justified by faith. But now that faith has come, we are no longer under a tutor. (Galatians 3:24-25)

They don't understand that Christ gives to those who trust in him everything they are trying to get by keeping his laws. He ends all of that. (Romans 10:4)

For if a law had been given which was able to impart life, then righteousness would indeed have been based on law. (Galatians 5:21)

This is the only thing I want to find out from you: did you receive the Spirit by the works of the Law, or by hearing with faith? Are you so foolish? Having begun by the Spirit, are you now being perfected by the flesh? (Galatians 3:2-3)

It was for freedom that Christ set us free; therefore keep standing firm and do not be subject again to a yoke of slavery. (Galatians 5:1)

Do you see why you had to die to the law? Because the law, summarized in the Ten Commandments, had a specific purpose. Its job was to show you that you were a sinner, and in need of a Savior. But once that job was done, once you were joined to me, you were no longer under the law. You died to it. *You couldn't be under it,* not if I was to be the one living in and through you.

Do you see why? You can either trust in your efforts to keep laws and rules, or you can trust me to be living my life through you. You can't do both.

You can choose to put yourself under law, but there's no life there. No law can give you life, because only I am the life. The law will have the same effect on you as before. Only this time it won't show you that you are a guilty sinner. It will show that you are a failing saint—failing through your self-effort.

I delivered you from all that. You died to the law so that you could be joined to me. So that you could be one spirit with me. So that I could come live inside you, and through you live my perfect life of love. I produce my own fruit through you now. It comes from me.

And what, on your end, is the operating principle of this life? Faith. It all comes by faith. You receive by faith. You don't receive through your self-effort to keep laws or rules.

The incredible news is that I brought you out of what is not life, into the wonder of me. I don't ask you to produce a life pleasing to the Father. I live a life pleasing to him already. I live it in you, through you, as you. Receive that. Simply receive.

Now to Him who is able to keep you from stumbling, and to make you stand in the presence of His glory blameless with great joy ... (Jude 24)

... He [Jesus] who was born of God keeps him [from sin], and the evil one does not touch him. (1 John 5:18)

For we do not have a high priest who cannot sympathize with our weaknesses, but One who has been tempted in all things as we are, yet without sin. (Hebrews 4:15)

LESSON 18

BECAUSE WE ARE ONE, WHEN
YOU ARE TEMPTED, I KEEP YOU

S o if you don't live by rules, and you don't live by your own self-effort, what is going to keep you from sinning?

I am. I keep you. You are kept by my power in you.

Not that I am going to override your will. But you and I are one. I am the One living this life in you, and sin has no power over me. Temptation is for my glory, and for yours as well. You have nothing to fear from it.

So let's get several things straight about temptation. First, it's never wrong that you are tempted. Temptation is a normal part of this human experience. In fact, it is part of a *perfect* human life. I was tempted in every way when I lived on earth. Was I wrong to be tempted?

Temptation is an important part of this life. I express myself mightily through you in times of temptation. And I use temptation, and even your failures, to press you into knowing me as your complete sufficiency. So, just as with other trials, you can actually rejoice in temptations.

Second, there is never any condemnation for you. Certainly there is no condemnation for being tempted. But neither is there any condemnation if you do sin. It is forgiven. We aren't separated in any way. Just acknowledge your sin and turn once again to me in faith.

Third, the key to living when you are tempted is the same as any other time: faith. I am the One living in you. You relax into me doing it. You live in the glorious freedom of my over-

For the death that He died, He died to sin once for all; but the life that He lives, He lives to God. (Romans 6:10)

For sin shall not be master over you, for you are not under law but under grace. (Romans 6:14)

coming life.

Sin deceives you into thinking it still dwells in your inmost being. It doesn't. You are born of God. But it often feels as if it does, and that the real "you" wants to disobey God. So you think you have to struggle to suppress what the real "you" allegedly wants.

It's all a lie. Your heart is on my side, regardless of what your feelings and appetites may be shouting to you. I know that.

But if you think it's the real you wanting to sin, you will be thrown back into independent, self-reliant living. It will seem as if we are separated, me up here, you down there, with you struggling as hard as you can against sin. That's not how you were designed to live. It's a setup for failure. You aren't kept by self-effort. You are kept by me. You trust me.

So you simply relax back into me. You live by grace, not law. And what does grace mean? I do it, you receive it. I am living in you, through you, as you. And this temptation is no match for me. I keep you. You say, "Lord, I am dead to sin and alive to you. You always live to the Father through me. How are you living through me in that way this moment?"

As you affirm the truth, and rest in me, the Spirit confirms. The Spirit empowers. You follow your heart's desire—to enjoy your oneness with me. And I manifest myself through you.

You have nothing to fear from your human appetites. You have died to them as your source of life. I know they have tripped you up many times in the past. But I am your life now. I have redeemed your appetites. I use them for my glory, to live my perfect life of love through you, to others. You are completely free. You can live spontaneously in your freedom, without fear.

Nor do you have anything to fear from the random thoughts and emotions that are a normal part of your human experi-

"I have been crucified with Christ; and it is no longer I who live, but Christ lives in me ... (Galatians 2:20)

ence. You are going to have thoughts that seem contrary to me. You are going to have feelings that seem contrary to me. They may seem very strong. But they are not the deepest part of you. Thoughts and feelings come and go. In your new heart, you are established. You and I are one. You want what I want.

Like temptations, your various thoughts and feelings are faith opportunities. They direct you to me. You affirm that I am the One living in you, manifesting myself through you. As you.

"My food is to do the will of Him who sent Me and to accomplish His work." — Jesus (John 4:34)

"I do not seek My own will, but the will of Him who sent Me." — Jesus (John 5:30)

For I joyfully concur with the law of God in the inner man ... (Romans 7:22)

Because we are one, we both delight to do our Father's will

My Father is my delight. I am his delight. His delight, for all eternity, is to glorify me. My delight, for all eternity, is to glorify him. I glorify him by doing his will. When I was on earth, my supreme delight, and my glory, was simply to do his will. I never sought anything other than what he wanted. It wasn't a sacrifice to do his will. It was my joy. That's all I came to do.

Now, I live in you. And my delight is exactly the same: to do his will, in you, through you, as you. It's all that I do, for he and I are one.

The wonder of your new birth is this: now the Father, and I, and the Spirit, are your delight as well. And you delight in my Father's will. Your supreme delight is doing his will, just as mine is. You may not know that yet. Many times it doesn't feel as if it's true. But in the depths of your being, in your inner man, you delight in what the Father wants. Because everything he wants, and I want, is good, and loving, and perfect.

So you and I are completely on the same page. We are one, and we function as one. Through you, I live my life, always doing the Father's will.

But you have been given your own human will, haven't you? That is how we created you. That is the honor, the incredible dignity, we have given you, to be created in our image, and be able to choose. And, even as his child, you can choose not to

"I glorified You on the earth, having accomplished the work which You have given Me to do. Now, Father, glorify Me together with Yourself, with the glory which I had with You before the world was." — prayer of Jesus (John 17:4-5)

For what the Law could not do, weak as it was through the flesh, God did: sending His own Son in the likeness of sinful flesh and as an offering for sin, He condemned sin in the flesh … (Romans 8:3)

Those who belong to Christ Jesus have crucified the flesh with its passions and desires. (Galatians 5:24)

do the Father's will, can't you? You can temporarily choose to live as if you are independent of our union. So how are you to think about that reality?

I realize that often you have thoughts or feelings that don't seem to be on board with what the Father wants. That's OK—I had those thoughts and feelings too! That's merely part of being human. My thoughts and feelings weren't on board before I went to the cross. I didn't *feel* like going to the cross. I was *thinking* about not going to the cross. I was even *asking* my Father if there was a way I could avoid going to the cross. So feeling and thinking and even asking are not wrong, because they are not the deepest part of who you are. In your deepest part, your inner man, you always delight to do the Father's will. As for your ability to think and feel, that is God-given. Remember, your humanity is my asset, not my liability. I created you this way, so that you and I could enjoy eternity together, and that I could express myself through you, just as you are.

I also realize that you still carry around something called the flesh, a propensity to seek life independently of me. The flesh isn't you. It's *never* the real you. It's not who you are in your new inner man. But it's still with you, because you live in an unredeemed body that has been programmed to seek life on its own. The flesh is linked to that body. That's why it's called *flesh*. One day you will eject from this mortal body and flesh won't be an issue anymore.

There's absolutely no condemnation for the flesh (since it's not who you are and since it's deeds were judged at the cross already) and, despite how it may feel to you, the flesh has no real power over you. Just as, on the cross, you died to sin and died to the law, you died to the flesh having any control of you.

But, on occasion, you will allow the flesh to deceive you into believing that you delight in something other than the Father's

It is God who works in you both to will and to do for His good pleasure. (Philippians 2:13)

"Come to Me, all who are weary and heavy-laden, and I will give you rest. Take My yoke upon you and learn from Me, for I am gentle and humble in heart, and you will find rest for your souls. For My yoke is easy and My burden is light." — Jesus (Matthew 11:28-30)

will, and you will start doing flesh's thing. When you do, our union is not affected. In fact, you take me with you in doing that thing. But it's not me doing it. If you rob a bank, it's not the bank-robber-Jesus in you doing it!

So you have the ability to think and feel (which is from me), but those thoughts and feelings don't always correspond to what the Father (and your inner man) wants. And you have the flesh (which is not from me, and is not even you), which has no power over you but is deceptive, inviting you to do its thing. How are you going to live with this reality? Are you going to be constantly looking at yourself, asking, "Is this me doing this, or is this Jesus?" No! That's an introspective dead end. We are one, which means you can't separate us out in that way.

You live with this reality just as with everything else: completely by faith in me. I have orchestrated all of this to press you into a walk of pure faith. You affirm what I say: You *do* delight in the Father's will. I *am* the One living in you, and I delight in the Father's will. We both do.

All of these things teach you to relax into me, fully depending on me. As you do, I am not only living through you, but I am at work in you, both to will and to do according to my good pleasure. And what is my good pleasure? To fully live through you, expressing every aspect of my being as you.

This is true joy, simply wanting what I want, and what the Father wants, and seeing me living that in you. It is life made simple. It is the rest that only I give. As with everything else, you just receive it.

... Christ is all, and in all. (Colossians 3:11)

And my God will supply all your needs according to His riches in glory in Christ Jesus. (Philippians 4:19)

... His divine power has granted to us everything pertaining to life and godliness ... (2 Peter 1:3)

But we have this treasure in earthen vessels, so that the surpassing greatness of the power will be of God and not from ourselves. (2 Corinthians 4:7)

"I am the bread of life; he who comes to Me will not hunger, and he who believes in Me will never thirst." — Jesus (John 6:35)

BECAUSE WE ARE ONE, I AM YOUR COMPLETE SUFFICIENCY

So what is the secret to this life? What is the key?

I am. I am your everything. I am your complete sufficiency. I am the total life in you, through you.

This life is not me plus anything. It's not me plus your effort, your discipline, your prayer life, your Bible study, your fellowship group, your ministry, or anything else you may rely on. Nor is this life me coming alongside you and helping you.

It's just me. I am the life. I live my life in you.

You already have me. You can't get more of me. You can't get closer to me. You can't do anything "spiritual" to get closer, or get more. You are complete, just as you are.

Nor are you hungering or thirsting for more. I have quenched your thirst. I have satisfied your hunger. You are full. That's what I told you, remember? Just affirm it. "Lord, you have quenched my thirst. You have satisfied my hunger. I may not feel it, but you have filled my every need. You are my complete fulfillment."

In his time, and in his way, the Spirit will confirm it in you. You affirm, you stand in faith, and the Spirit will confirm what is already true. You experience *what already is* by faith.

I am your supply. You died to trying to meet your needs on your own. You aren't here to fend for yourself any longer. I am your eternal need-meeter. I have already supplied every provision for your life—spiritual, emotional, physical, material. I have provided for all your needs. How could it be otherwise? You and I are one. How could I let myself go unprovided for?

But by His doing you are in Christ Jesus, who became to us wisdom from God, and righteousness and sanctification, and redemption … (1 Corinthians 1:30)

And He has said to me, "My grace is sufficient for you, for power is perfected in weakness." Most gladly, therefore, I will rather boast about my weaknesses, so that the power of Christ may dwell in me. Therefore I am well content with weaknesses, with insults, with distresses, with persecutions, with difficulties, for Christ's sake; for when I am weak, then I am strong. (2 Corinthians 12:9-10)

For as many as are the promises of God, in [Christ] they are yes … (2 Corinthians 1:20)

"My sheep hear My voice …" — Jesus (John 10:27a)

For all who are being led by the Spirit of God, these are sons of God. (Romans 8:14)

I am the head; you are the body. Am I not going to provide for my own body?

I have, in fact, *already* supplied everything you need. I am enthroned, right now, in that area of need you have. I have allowed the need to appear for the purpose of supplying it. Faith sees the Supplier, who has already supplied the need. In me, all the Father's promises to you are *already* "yes."

I, living in you, am adequate for every situation. My overcoming life in you is adequate for every circumstance, no matter how it looks from an earthly perspective. You feel weak. You feel inadequate. You don't feel wise enough. You don't have the love you need. Of course you don't! You're not meant to. If I come to live in a vessel that is weak, I *have* to be the strength. If you lack wisdom, I *have* to be the wisdom. If you are inadequate, I *have* to be your adequacy. I have to be the love in you. I have to be the forgiveness in you. And I am. Always.

You live simply by the awareness of Another living in you. By complete dependence on Another. You recognize that all that you do is me doing it through you.

Not even your faith, your recognition, your awareness, comes through self-effort. It's the work of my Spirit in you. You simply acknowledge the reality of who I am in you. You affirm. My Spirit confirms in you. Your role is to be willing. Your willingness is expressed as faith.

My Spirit governs you now. He leads you. You hear my voice. You are my sheep. You don't have to work at hearing my voice. You *do* hear it. That's what I told you. Rest in that.

See me—in you—with a single eye. I am the All in you. Don't look at yourself and how you think you need to improve. You can't make that happen anyway. Turn your attention completely to the One whom you contain, who lives through you. I am your complete sufficiency. I always will be.

... much more those who receive the abundance of grace and of the gift of righteousness will reign in life through the One, Jesus Christ. (Romans 5:17)

What then shall we say to these things? If God is for us, who is against us? He who did not spare His own Son, but delivered Him over for us all, how will He not also with Him freely give us all things? (Romans 8:31-32)

Not that I speak from want, for I have learned to be content in whatever circumstances I am. (Philippians 4:11)

LESSON 21

BECAUSE WE ARE ONE,
YOU REIGN IN LIFE

I said once through the Apostle Paul that those who receive my abundant grace, and my gift of righteousness, reign in life. You have received my gift of righteousness. You receive each day my abundant grace. You reign in life.

You have thought of this life as something that you live, maybe with my help. It isn't. It's something that I live in you. You can never live this life. You were never meant to. Only I am the life.

Until you know this, life seems all about your activity. What are the things you are supposed to do? What are the things you are supposed to avoid? How can you finally get spiritual enough, on board with the program?

But this life isn't about your activity. It's about your receptivity. You receive me as the One living in you, through you, as you. Any activity on your part simply flows from that.

Do you see how incredibly freeing this is?

You are no longer focused on improving your performance. You are no longer focused on your performance at all. I am the One living in you. I am the One living through you. If anyone's performance is being focused on, it is only mine. How am I doing?

You don't live a life of worry. I have provided all your needs. You don't live a life of struggle. I am the overcomer in you. You don't live a life of lovelessness. I am the love in you. You don't live a life of bitterness. I am the forgiveness in you. You don't

... and though you have not seen Him, you love Him, and though you do not see Him now, but believe in Him, you greatly rejoice with joy inexpressible and full of glory. (1 Peter 1:8)

... the peace of God, which surpasses all comprehension ... (Philippians 4:7)

... always giving thanks for all things in the name of our Lord Jesus Christ to God, even the Father. (Ephesians 5:20)

live a life of feeling bad about yourself, measuring yourself by worldly standards or even your own expectations. I have made you completely acceptable and pleasing to me, just as you are.

You are perfectly loved, perfectly accepted, perfectly provided for, perfectly protected, perfectly guided. What can be against you?

You live with peace, with joy, with genuine love for others, for you have been freed to give freely to them. You aren't grasping what they can give you anymore. You are full. Your life is now completely available to others. You are free to be a conduit of my love to them: my acceptance, my provision, my life. You don't see their clay feet, their many imperfections. You see me in them. Your true reward is seeing my life flow out through you to others, until I am formed in them.

You live in my rest. You have ceased from your own self-effort. You have ceased from your own works. You've stopped seeking personal revival or more commitment from yourself. You already have it all. I am the One living through you.

Trials are no longer a burden to you. In truth, they are an adventure, in which you see me expressing myself to this broken world. You rejoice in trials.

Temptations are no longer a threat. They are an opportunity to experience my sufficiency in you. I am your victory.

Circumstances are not obstacles to your plans. They are the places I have chosen to express myself through you. Now, you give thanks in all things, and for all things. You rejoice, always.

You no longer live in fear and anxiety. You are completely free. You are completely provided for. You are completely depending on Another to be everything through you. You simply receive.

You don't even fear failure. I will redeem your failures, using them to bring you or others into the fullness of my life.

For we who have believed enter that rest ... For the one who has entered His rest has himself also rested from his works, as God did from His. (Hebrews 4:3, 10)

"I have been crucified with Christ; and it is no longer I who live, but Christ lives in me ..." (Galatians 2:20)

Now, you have a brand new reality in your life. You have something genuinely transforming, a reality that people are drawn to: not a life of religious striving, but One who lives his always sufficient, always victorious, always fulfilling life in you. This life is already yours. I already live in you, through you, as you. You simply receive it. You affirm what is already true. You keep affirming; you keep trusting according to the faith I have given you. It is my work to confirm, to bring inner knowing, to fully reveal myself in you. You don't even strive to believe. You relax into me. I am the Believer in you. You live by my faith.

There is nothing you can do to add to my perfect life in you. I am your All. I am being your All right now.

You reign in life. You are already seated with me, right now, in the heavenlies. You are being prepared to reign with me forever. You are now the light of the world. I shine through you.

Because we are one.

Just as I always planned we would be, for all eternity.

EPILOGUE

GROWING INTO FULLNESS

The lessons appeared twice a week for about ten weeks. Then they stopped. I guess I understood why. My life had been transformed. I had changed.

Or, perhaps more accurately, I had grown. I had come to understand that God wasn't in the business of changing me, as if I was unacceptable. He was in the process of maturing me—growing me up into the fullness of who I already was.

That was already happening in me. I was growing in my awareness of Christ living in me, through me, as me every day. More and more, the Spirit was causing me to know. I was being led by the Spirit. That is how sons live.

Still, I missed the lessons. Who wouldn't?

Three Saturdays after I received lesson 21, I went to Starbucks to meet with Tim. He had flown in from Abu Dhabi a couple of nights before. I hadn't told him about the envelopes. I'd just mentioned that God had been using some material in my life.

Tim and I caught up on the prior three months. "It wasn't miserable!" he insisted. "But I am very glad to be home."

After a while, I put a piece of paper on the table. Tim glanced at it. "Hey, this is what you mentioned in your email, isn't it? The material God is using in your life." He read the first few sentences. "It's in the first person—like a letter from Jesus."

"Right."

"That would really be something, to get a letter from Jesus."

"It would, wouldn't it?"

"Who gave these to you?"

"God did."

He smiled, unknowing. "Well, all things are from him, aren't they?"

Tim and I started going through the lessons together, one a week. I started seeing him grow into the fullness of being a son. Just as I was.

Jesus left Starbucks that Saturday and drove back to my house. Or rather, I did. No, we both did. I pulled into the driveway and walked across the grass to the front door, where I paused. There, leaning against the door frame, was a manila envelope. Handwritten on the outside were these words:

Dylan,
You are My treasure

I opened the envelope. Inside was another lesson. I took it inside, went to the breakfast table, and read it. And when I finished, I just sat back, amazed. Because I realized the lesson spoke to a deep question that I had—maybe the deepest. And what amazed me was that I didn't even know that I had it. But Jesus knew.

There weren't any questions at the end of this lesson. And I thought I knew why. I had come to know that the Answer lived inside me. I was one with him, forever. I was his treasure. What else did I need?

... just as [God] chose us in [Christ] before the foundation of the world, that we would be holy and blameless before Him. (Ephesians 1:4)

... the Lamb slain from the foundation of the world. (Revelation 13:8)

Although [Jesus] existed in the form of God, [He] did not regard equality with God a thing to be grasped, but emptied Himself, taking the form of a bond-servant, and being made in the likeness of men. Being found in appearance as a man, He humbled Himself by becoming obedient to the point of death, even death on a cross. (Philippians 2:6-8)

[God] made [Jesus] who knew no sin to be sin on our behalf, so that we might become the righteousness of God in Him. (2 Corinthians 5:21)

YOU ARE MY TREASURE

You are my treasure.

Do you want to know how you can be sure of that?

Before I created a single atom, before the universe ever began, I had you in mind. I chose you. Everything I created, I created with this end in mind: that I would have you.

But not just that. Before the universe began, I knew—more than that, I planned—that one day I would come to earth and pay the ultimate price. For what? To get you.

So I came. I, the One who made everything, to whom all things owe their being, whom all the heavens worship without end—I chose to become human. I took on a mortal, limited body. I entered a world filled with sin, and disease, and decay, and sorrow, and filth, and I chose to live in that world. I laid aside all my divine privileges. I shed all my right to be worshiped and adored. Instead, I was mocked, smeared, laughed at, dismissed, attacked, and rejected. I lived here as a man, to fully taste the horror of what sin had done to my creation.

Why did I stoop so unimaginably low? To get you.

I then chose the ultimate horror: death on a cross. But not just physical death. I became hideous, loathsome, vile sin itself. In doing so, I was, for the only time in all eternity, separated from the Father. The connection I had enjoyed with him from eternity past was lost. He poured out his full wrath against sin on me.

Why did I suffer so incredibly? To get you.

But it was impossible for death to hold me. I rose from the dead, and ascended, and am seated in the heavenlies, reigning

He was despised and forsaken of men, a man of sorrows and acquainted with grief; and like one from whom men hide their face He was despised, and we did not esteem Him ... He was pierced through for our transgressions, He was crushed for our iniquities ... (Isaiah 53:3, 5)

"I have manifested Your name to the men whom You gave Me out of the world; they were Yours and You gave them to Me ... I ask on their behalf; I do not ask on behalf of the world, but of those Whom You have given Me ..." — prayer of Jesus (John 17:6, 9)

For no one ever hated his own flesh, but nourishes and cherishes it, just as Christ also does the church, because we are members of His body. (Ephesians 5:29-30)

"I have loved you with an everlasting love; therefore I have drawn you with lovingkindness." (Jeremiah 31:3)

forever. And do you know who is already seated there with me? You are.

My Father has given you to me. Do you realize what that makes you? A gift. You are the ultimate gift from the Father to me. You are the gift he has planned to give me for all eternity.

Do you see why you are my treasure?

Do you think that what puny flesh may do in this brief time on earth, or whatever failures you may see in yourself as you live in these brief moments, can in any way stop you from being my treasure?

We talked at the very beginning of these lessons about how human love, even at its purest, is but a poor reflection of the perfect, infinite love of God. Has it ever occurred to you that human passion is this way, too?

Haven't you read the incredible passion of the two lovers for one another in the Song of Songs? They are consumed with their love for each other. Don't you realize that theirs is but a poor reflection of a higher, eternal passion? Don't you understand that my love is far more passionate than human love could ever be?

You are my treasure. You are my passion.

I have been waiting for all eternity to join myself to you. To join you to myself, and the Father, and the Spirit. Now that has become reality. Soon, we will celebrate our joining. All of heaven will celebrate. And we will never stop celebrating.

I will never stop celebrating, because you are my treasure. You will never stop celebrating, because I am yours.

QUESTIONS

Oh, I almost forgot. Here are the questions that came with each of the lessons.

LESSON 1

1. Have you ever thought of God as infinitely happy? What does it mean for your life that I am the infinitely happy God?
2. If the life that I have given you is quite simple, but it has seemed very complicated, what could have made it seem that way?
3. Look at the list of things I didn't create you for. How have you been living as if one or more things on that list *is* what I have created you for?
4. How have you believed, or operated as if, my love is somehow like human love?
5. What is the implication for your life that your primary purpose is to enjoy something? What is it you were created to enjoy?

LESSON 2

1. What in your life tells you that striving to make life work isn't what you were created for?
2. How does what you were created for—being one with me—make striving unnecessary?
3. Why is it that keeping rules and performing rituals can't make anyone one with me?
4. In what ways are you living as if your purpose is to strive to attain the right behavior?
5. What would it be like if, instead of your striving, someone else produced that right behavior in you?
6. Why would being one with the infinitely happy, infinitely loving God fulfill your heart's true desires?

LESSON 3

1. If the whole reason you were created was to be one with me, what was the ultimate effect of sin in your life, and the life of every human?
2. Is there anything you personally could do to solve that problem? Why or why not?
3. What was the real reason I wanted to take care of the sin issue between us?
4. Why is it that I could pay for the sins of all of humanity?
5. Why can forgiveness of your sins only be received as a gift, not as something you can earn?

LESSON 4

1. What kind of spiritual heart were you born into this world with? How would you describe it?
2. Why did I have to give you a heart transplant?
3. What kind of heart is your new heart? How would you describe it?

4. What kind of person does this make you in your deepest being?

5. How do I relate to this new person whom I have given birth to?

LESSON 5

1. What does it mean to be one spirit with me?

2. How does such a oneness come about, and who brings it about?

3. What is your role in this process of becoming one with me? What do you have to do?

4. Have you done that? If so, when and how? If not, what is stopping you from doing it right now?

5. What does it now mean for your life, that you are one with me?

LESSON 6

1. What are your chances of successfully replicating my life through your own effort? What does that say about living your life?

2. In what ways have you operated on the belief that you initially received me by faith, but after that you had to live by works, by your own self-effort?

3. Explain why that isn't true, and why it doesn't work.

4. What does it mean that I am living my life through you? How is that possible?

LESSON 7

1. What do I mean when I say I can't give you patience, kindness, etc.? Why can't I?

2. How today have you been trying to produce the life that only I can produce? How about this year?

3. What things in life try to convince you that you should produce the life yourself? What messages do they give you?
4. If I am the everything in you, and you are confronted with a negative situation, negative thoughts, or negative feelings, what is your role in me living through you?
5. Why is it incredibly freeing for you to simply be a container?

LESSON 8
1. In what ways do you put pressure on yourself to produce spiritual fruit?
2. How has that worked for you? What does that effort actually produce?
3. Can you see all of my life, when I lived on the earth, as the Father living through me? If as I am, so also are you in this world (1 John 4:17), what does this mean for you?
4. If deep down you are completely acceptable right now, what does that change in your life?
5. How can you simultaneously be completely acceptable and *also* be weak, unable to produce my life through your own effort? Is there any contradiction in that? Why not?
6. Based on what I have said in this lesson, what are you going to choose to receive by faith?

LESSON 9
1. Why have I designed our union relationship to be one of me producing and you receiving?
2. What's the difference between your faith creating the reality and your faith acknowledging the reality that is already there?
3. What is the already-there reality that I am calling you to trust in?

4. How might that have applied to a specific incident in your life today?

5. What does it mean for you to live by *my* faith?

LESSON 10

1. According to 1 Corinthians 2:12, what is the Spirit's job in you? What, primarily, is he going to show you?

2. What is it that produces knowing in you—you, or the thing you are putting your faith in? Explain.

3. What is your role in cooperating in this process of knowing?

4. What is the obedience of faith?

5. What are you going to declare by faith today, and keep declaring?

6. What are the "appearances to the contrary" to this declaration? How are you going to respond to those appearances to the contrary?

LESSON 11

1. If God is love, and love is self-giving, why is it significant that God is three Persons instead of one? Who could each Person love before creation?

2. If I am producing my life in you, what is the nature of that life going to be? How would you describe it?

3. Is it possible to be filled by me and yet have feelings that don't always feel fulfilled? Explain.

4. What does it mean that you have died to being a self-getter?

5. What are you going to receive by faith, and affirm, as a result of this lesson?

LESSON 12

1. How *could* I have chosen to see the cross as I approached being crucified? What evil could I have focused on? Who could I have blamed?
2. How did I choose to see the cross instead? What was the result of that choice?
3. What are some difficult circumstances in your life right now? Do those circumstances appear good or bad to you? How am I seeing those circumstances?
4. Why is seeing your circumstances as I see them a gift? Can you choose to receive that gift today in each of your current circumstances?
5. What circumstances in your past do you need to receive this gift for?
6. Can you praise me for working in your present (or past) circumstances for good in your life and the lives of others?

LESSON 13

1. I say that you are a righteous new creation. Your behavior sometimes says that you are still a sinner. Who are you going to choose to believe? Why?
2. How is it possible that your old man was actually crucified on the cross with me, and your new man raised with me?
3. What change did this make in who you are?
4. How does it change how you think about yourself, your life, and your relationship with me if you are a holy, righteous, complete new creation instead of a sinner?
5. What difference does it make in approaching me, and making your requests known to me, if you are perfectly righteous and already seated with me in the heavenlies, versus being a sinner?

LESSON 14

1. When I said at the cross, "It is finished," how much of the sin issue between you and God did I take care of? Fifty percent? Ninety percent?

2. In what ways have you continued to believe, and behave, as if the sin issue between us has not been completely removed?

3. Think about the fact that God doesn't ever deal with you anymore according to your sins. What difference does that make in how you relate to him? In how you relate to yourself? In how you live your life?

4. The animal sacrifices under the Law could never deliver the people from a sin consciousness. What have I done to deliver you from sin consciousness? What does it look like to live with a Christ consciousness instead of a sin consciousness?

5. Have you believed all this time that as a believer you aren't forgiven of your sins unless you continually confess them? Look at 1 John 1:9. Now look at the verses right before and after. Do verses 8 and 10 describe you? When was the last time you claimed to be sinless? John wrote to churches being infiltrated by Gnostics, who claimed to have no sin and therefore did not see their need to receive me as their Savior. In light of that, what might 1 John 1:8-10 actually mean? Does John say that believers' sins are forgiven or not? Look at 1 John 2:12, just a few verses later. What does Paul say? Look at Colossians 2:13. Once you have received me, do you really need to do anything to get your sins forgiven? Have I taken care of the sin issue between us or not?

157

LESSON 15

1. Why can there never be any separation between us now?
2. What does it mean for our relationship that there is never any separation? What does it mean for our relationship that we are not constantly hopping in and out of fellowship (sharing, participation)?
3. Do you still ever *feel* as if we are somehow separated or out of fellowship? What causes you to feel that way?
4. Given the truth about our oneness, how are you going to respond when you feel that way now?
5. What would happen if you got into a habit of confessing your righteousness, and our oneness?

LESSON 16

1. What causes you to believe that sin has power over you? Your experience? Who are you going to believe—your experience, or what I say? Why?
2. Look at Romans 6:6-7. Is there any doubt that your old man died at the cross? Is there any doubt that you have been freed from sin?
3. What does that mean, that you have been freed from sin?
4. If it's no longer you who sin, but sin which dwells in you, how does that change the way you see temptation?
5. How does trusting that I am the one living in you, and I always live to the Father, change your response to the pull of sin on you?
6. Have you been called to struggle to overcome sin, or to rest in faith and let me handle sin through you? Explain.

LESSON 17

1. What was the law's function?
2. Once it fulfilled that function, why did I have to kill you

off to it?

3. Why is it that, if I am the One living in you, I don't need laws and rules?
4. What are some of the rules that Christians tend to put themselves under?
5. What are some of the rules that, consciously or not, you personally tend to put yourself under?
6. How are you going to receive today the reality of me living my life in you, instead of you living by rules?

LESSON 18

1. How can temptation be part of a perfect human life?
2. How do I use temptation in your life to achieve my eternal purposes in you?
3. Why can victory over temptation only come through grace, not through law? What does grace actually mean?
4. Think about the battle between me, the living God, and the temptations of your bodily programming. Who do you think has the upper hand in that battle? Why?
5. What is the significance of the fact that there is no one in your deepest being who wants to sin? What difference does that make?
6. Do you think I fear your human appetites? Or have I given them to you for my intentional purposes, to use as I live through you? Explain how that might work.

LESSON 19

1. Who is My delight each day, from before the time there even were days?
2. Who is the delight of your new inner man?
3. Why can it feel as if other things are your delight?
4. Is there any condemnation for feeling those things?

5. Why is the flesh never the real you?

6. If I am the one living in you, and I delight perfectly in the Father, how are you going to enter into the reality of what I am already doing in you?

LESSON 20

1. How does this lesson run completely contrary to everything the world teaches you?

2. How does it run contrary to what religion teaches you?

3. How have you been living as if this life is me-plus-something? What have the "somethings" been for you?

4. I am your complete sufficiency, but are you always going to feel that? Why not?

5. How are you going to experience the reality of me being your complete sufficiency if you don't always feel that way?

6. Why did I put you into a life in which you feel weak, inadequate, and insufficient? Will you ever stop feeling that way? If not, how are you going to choose to live in the midst of it?

7. What does it mean to stop looking at yourself, or trying to improve yourself, and simply look to the One whom you contain?

LESSON 21

1. What have you received that enables you to reign in life? Are you now missing anything?

2. What is the difference between living by faith and living by self-effort? What does it mean that this life isn't about your activity, but your receptivity?

3. Why is it that I am not really here to help you? What am I here to do instead?

4. Why is it that you reign in life? Describe that kind of life.

SCRIPTURE REFERENCES

All Scripture quotations are taken from the New American Standard Bible® (NASB) except the following:

John 6:57 (English Standard Version)
John 17:21, 23, 26 (English Standard Version)
Romans 3:22-25 (New Living Translation)
Romans 10:4 (The Living Bible)
2 Corinthians 4:6-7 (New Living Translation)
2 Corinthians 4:7, 10-12 (New English Translation)
Galatians 2:20b (King James Version)
Philippians 4:13 (New King James Version)
1 Timothy 1:11 (John Piper, *The Pleasures of God*, p. 23)
Hebrews 11:1 (New King James Version)
Hebrews 12:7 (The Message)
1 John 1:4 (New Century Version)
1 John 4:10 (NET Bible)
1 John 5:20 (English Standard Version)
Revelation 13:8 (New King James Version)

ABOUT THE AUTHOR

The New York Times' bestselling author David Gregory has enthralled readers with "what-if" stories involving unexpected, life-changing encounters in seven novels, including *Dinner with a Perfect Stranger, Open,* and *The Last Christian.* He also coauthored the nonfiction *The Rest of the Gospel: When the Partial Gospel Has Worn You Out.* A native of Texas, David holds master's degrees from Dallas Theological Seminary and The University of North Texas and is a former writer and editor with Insight for Living, the Bible-teaching ministry of Charles Swindoll.

For more information about David, to invite him to speak, or to simply connect with him, find him at:

www.davidgregorybooks.com

 **facebook.com/DavidGregoryAuthor**

 **twitter.com/davidgregorys**

ALSO BY
DAVID GREGORY

Dinner with a Perfect Stranger: An Invitation Worth Considering

A Day with a Perfect Stranger

Night with a Perfect Stranger: The Conversation That Changes Everything

The Rest of the Gospel: When the Partial Gospel Has Worn You Out (with Dan Stone)

The Last Christian: A Novel

Open: Get Ready for the Adventure of a Lifetime

Patriot Rules: A Novel

The Next Level: A Parable of Finding Your Place in Life

If you were blessed by
If Jesus Loves Me Why Isn't This Working?
you will love
The Rest of the Gospel:
When the Partial Gospel Has Worn You Out
by Dan Stone and David Gregory

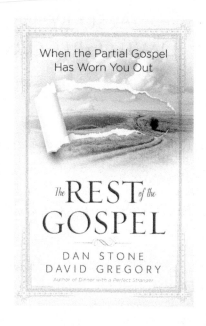

Having God's forgiveness is wonderful. Spending eternity with God is great. But for now, where is the abundant life Jesus promised? Why is the Christian life such a struggle? Because getting forgiven is only half of the gospel! *The Rest of the Gospel* is not us striving on our own to be "good" Christians, but Christ in us, living his life through us as we rest in him.